The ESSENCE of Autism and Other Neurodevelopmental Conditions

of related interest

Food Refusal and Avoidant Eating in Children, including those with Autism Spectrum Conditions
A Practical Guide for Parents and Professionals
Gillian Harris and Elizabeth Shea
ISBN 978 1 78592 318 0
eISBN 978 1 78450 632 2

PANDAS and PANS in School Settings
A Handbook for Educators
Edited by Patricia Rice Doran
Foreword by Diana Pohlman
ISBN 978 1 84905 744 8
eISBN 978 1 78450 166 2

Kids in the Syndrome Mix of ADHD, LD, Autism Spectrum, Tourette's, Anxiety, and More!
The one-stop guide for parents, teachers, and other professionals
Martin L. Kutscher, MD
With contributions from Tony Attwood, PhD and Robert R. Wolff, MD
ISBN 978 1 84905 967 1
eISBN 978 0 85700 882 4

Autism Spectrum Disorders Through the Life Span
Digby Tantam
Hardback ISBN 978 1 84310 993 8
Paperback ISBN 978 1 84905 344 0
eISBN 978 0 85700 511 3

The ESSENCE of Autism and Other Neurodevelopmental Conditions

Rethinking Co-Morbidities, Assessment, and Intervention

CHRISTOPHER GILLBERG

Jessica Kingsley Publishers
London and Philadelphia

First published in Great Britain in 2021 by Jessica Kingsley Publishers
An Hachette Company

1

Copyright © Christopher Gillberg 2021

Front cover image source: Christopher Gillberg.

A CIP catalogue record for this title is available from the
British Library and the Library of Congress

ISBN 978 1 78775 439 3
eISBN 978 1 78775 440 9

Printed and bound in the United States by Integrated Books International

Jessica Kingsley Publishers' policy is to use papers that are natural,
renewable and recyclable products and made from wood grown in
sustainable forests. The logging and manufacturing processes are expected
to conform to the environmental regulations of the country of origin.

Jessica Kingsley Publishers
Carmelite House
50 Victoria Embankment
London EC4Y 0DZ

www.jkp.com

Contents

Chapter 1

What Is ESSENCE?

It has long been known that intellectual disability (ID) tends to bring about major long-term adjustment problems, and in recent years autism (or autism spectrum disorder/ASD) has also come to be usually viewed as a severe functional impairment into adulthood. However, far fewer people recognize that early-onset concentration difficulties, planning issues, attention deficits, impulsiveness, and restlessness (nowadays sometimes diagnosed as attention-deficit/hyperactivity disorder/ADHD) can cause those affected to become social outcasts and experience additional psychiatric problems as early as from their teens. In fact, a large number of early developmental disorders among children – such as language disorder, developmental coordination disorder (DCD), perception disorders, "mild learning difficulties" (which in our day and age should not be taken lightly), conduct disorders, various tic-related conditions/syndromes, and early-onset mood swings (which may sometimes portend bipolar/manic-depressive disorder) – heavily increase the risk of significant mental health deterioration, school failure, social alienation, and serious criminal activity in adulthood (Gillberg 1995).

These abnormalities virtually always occur in groups of two or more. Today, in many countries, they lead to early consultations with nurses, paediatricians, psychologists, and speech and language therapists (Gillberg 2010; Hatakenaka *et al.* 2017). Usually, all attention is directed at only one specific aspect of the full set of problems (e.g. language delay), all the while missing the bigger picture and the serious prognostic implications involved. In order to provide tailored support and optimal treatment, one must focus on the totality of the child's difficulties and strengths from the very beginning.

The term ESSENCE

The problem with the umbrella terms typically used within the field – primarily in the areas of neuropsychiatry and neurodevelopment – is that they assume ADHD or autism, for example, to be the primary diagnosis and that comorbidity is *not* the rule. Moreover, it is illogical to address certain psychiatric problems as *neuro*psychiatric; all psychiatric problems originate in the brain and should thus be considered "neuro". The term "neurodevelopmental problems" is also misleading as it implies that the problems only exist during "development". ESSENCE (Early Symptomatic Syndromes Eliciting Neurodevelopmental Clinical Examinations), on the other hand, assumes that comorbidity is *always* present, that symptoms of one diagnostic category or the other could very well be identical at the beginning of the child's life, that it is not always possible to *permanently* decide which diagnosis should apply (even though it is necessary to address the issues as a real problem requiring an actual name), and that one or the other (ADHD or autism) could be more salient at different times during development (Gillberg 2010, 2014). For example, it is not uncommon for a child to initially, at the age of 3 years, seem to *primarily* have autism, only to eventually fit the criteria for ADHD much better at the age of 10 years (even if the autistic symptoms linger, they are no longer as much of an impediment as the symptoms that warrant an ADHD diagnosis).

The term "ESSENCE" is also neutral in the sense that it does not "take sides" with regard to neuropsychiatry or neurodevelopment, but merely highlights the link between early-onset symptomatic conditions and clinical examinations.

Applying ESSENCE in practice means, for example, that every child with several autistic symptoms and every child with pronounced ADHD symptoms must be examined with regard to other problems

8

included under the ESSENCE umbrella. Furthermore, ESSENCE promotes the idea that children and families need early assistance from one single cohesive unit/facility, preferably a multiprofessional team consisting of doctors, psychologists, nurses, educators, and speech and language therapists (as well as a number of additional professional groups that should always be included in such teams).

The knowledge development regarding what is here referred to as ESSENCE has been going on worldwide for the last 45 years. New clinical methods (e.g. questionnaires, diagnostic interviews, and structured observation methods), long-term follow-up, and research into neuropsychology (new tests and refinement of older ones), genetics, epigenetics, neurochemistry, neurophysiology, and brain imaging, as well as a growing consensus on how different conditions should be differentiated from (and grouped with) one another, have all led to a completely new understanding of how ESSENCE in many cases contributes to explaining lifetime prognoses of school failure and professional failure, as well as high rates of poor mental health, drug abuse, and criminal behaviour. Both new and old intervention and treatment methods have been evaluated in a systematic manner, which has led to the development of effective intervention measures based on scientific research and proven experience. One research group at the Gillberg Neuropsychiatry Centre at the University of Gothenburg – with collaborators across large parts of the world – has in many cases been at the forefront of this process. This short book presents an overview of the ESSENCE term and the components/syndromes it encompasses.

Table 1.1 Early Symptomatic Syndromes Eliciting Neurodevelopmental Clinical Examinations (ESSENCE)

Syndrome	Prevalence	References
Autism spectrum disorder (ASD)	1.0	Coleman & Gillberg 2012; Lundström et al. 2015
Attention-deficit/hyperactivity disorder (ADHD)	3.7–5.0	Kadesjö & Gillberg 2001; Faraone et al. 2003
Tourette's syndrome	1.1	Kadesjö & Gillberg 2000

Syndrome	Prevalence	References
Intellectual disability (ID)	2.5	Gillberg & Söderström 2003
Speech and language disorder	4.0	Miniscalco *et al.* 2006
Developmental coordination disorder (DCD)	4.9	Kadesjö & Gillberg 1999
Reactive attachment disorder (RAD) and disinhibited social engagement disorder (DSED)	0.5–1.5	Sadiq *et al.* 2012; Minnis *et al.* 2013
Selective mutism	0.2–2.0	Kopp & Gillberg 1997
Severe early-onset affective disorders	?	Biederman *et al.* 2003
Paediatric acute-onset neuropsychiatric syndrome (PANS) Paediatric autoimmune neuropsychiatric disorders associated with streptococcal infection (PANDAS)	?	Johnson *et al.* 2019
Behavioural phenotype syndromes (BPS)	2.0	Gillberg 2010
Epilepsy with other ESSENCE	0.5	Aicardi 2009
Total prevalence/overlap accounted for	c. 10.0	Gillberg 2010

Prevalence of ESSENCE

The total rate of early – which is to say upon entering school or earlier – diagnosable ESSENCE (sometimes also referred to as child neuropsychiatric or neurodevelopmental disorders/impairments/variations) is about 10 per cent of the population (probably around 13% of all boys and 7% cent of all girls). In many countries, about half of these children (probably 8% of all boys but only 2% of all girls) have already shown up before age 10 years at some kind of healthcare clinic and been examined by a doctor, psychologist, or speech and language therapist, often with a resulting diagnosis of "language disorder", "developmental delay", or "autism". Quite often, the conclusion at an early age is that there is some unspecified abnormality in the child's development, but no diagnosis given for it. In other cases, parents might get some reassuring news (e.g. at the autism clinic where they are told "it's not autism, so there isn't anything for us to deal with") or be told to "wait and see". The remaining half will be detected as "problematic cases" before reaching adulthood and then often given diagnoses such as ADHD, depression, "anxiety", or "family relationship problems". Rarely if ever is the family made aware from the outset that the child has a complex set of problems which wholly or partially meet criteria for several of the neurodevelopmental diagnoses indicated in the diagnostic manuals used in healthcare services, such as the DSM (*Diagnostic and Statistical Manual of Mental Disorders/DSM-5*, APA 2013) or ICD (*International Classification of Diseases/ICD-11*, World Health Organization 2018).

When should one suspect ESSENCE?

Children showing signs of abnormal development, behavioural disorder, or mood swings/problems severe enough that they cause the parents or others in the child's environment to feel concerned very often have ESSENCE-related problems. The symptoms and concerns have been present for many months (or appeared suddenly, over the course of just a few days, in a child who initially showed completely "normal" development). All children with long-term (or extremely acute-onset) problems of the kinds listed in Table 1.2 should be subjected to some kind of developmental evaluation (Gillberg 2018).

Table 1.2 Problems that have led to concerns for many months and that might indicate ESSENCE

Concern regarding child's development	Example
General development	Late
Motor – movement	Poor coordination, delayed, low muscle tone, little mimicry
Communication – speech	Little babbling, delayed or no speech, monotone

Concern regarding child's development	Example
Social interaction – contact	Little or no interaction, does not initiate contact
Activity – impulsivity	Extremely active or inactive, extremely impulsive
Attention – concentration	Flimsy, never there, in his own world, cannot concentrate
Behaviour	Stereotypical movements, cannot tolerate routine change
Mood	Extreme mood instability
Sleep	Extreme sleep disturbance that has lasted many months
Feeding	Major feeding problems that have lasted many months
Sensory reaction	Over- or underreacting to sounds, smells, light, touch, pain, heat, cold, etc.

Outcome

Through long-term follow-up of children with any of the diagnoses of autism, language disorder, intellectual disability, learning problems, or ADHD, we now know that in many cases the fundamental problems outlined in these diagnoses (social interaction difficulties, communication problems, learning difficulties, reading and writing difficulties/dyslexia, motor coordination problems, and attention disorders) remain into adulthood, even in those cases (just under half of all affected) where all diagnostic criteria necessary to obtain the diagnosis are no longer met. We also know that the mortality rate is elevated, even though the vast majority will live to old age.

Taken together, these numbers tell us that at least 5 per cent of the adult population still have diagnosable ESSENCE problems even in adulthood and that several additional per cent have underlying problems that cause them continued functional impediments. The majority of adults with ESSENCE also meet criteria for additional diagnoses – depression, anxiety, pain disorder, personality disorder (antisocial, avoidant, borderline, etc.), and drug addiction. A rather significant portion go on to early retirement, unemployment benefits, or welfare. A large group of all affected with ADHD (perhaps 20%) end up in criminal care (where 30–70% of all inmates may have ADHD), generally due to impulsive violent crimes or drug-related crime.

It should also be noted that there are "good" outcomes in cases of autism and Tourette's syndrome, primarily in cases where families have been provided with early diagnosis, information, and some degree of subsequent support. Many individuals in these groups have a strong artistic aptitude, think "outside the box", and can be generally creative. Both those who are extremely impulsive (e.g. in cases of ADHD and Tourette's syndrome) and those who are extremely compulsive (e.g. in cases of autism) can, in the best possible cases and with tailored support, develop into entrepreneurs, artists of different kinds, and scientific researchers.

Structure of the book

From this point on, one chapter will be devoted to each of the so-called syndromes included under the umbrella term of ESSENCE. "Syndrome" in this context refers to deviations from whatever is considered normal variation and that manifest as certain symptoms occurring together in a relatively predictable manner. Each of the syndromes will be addressed individually and separately from the others. In reality, however, "pure" cases are rare. One example of this is that about 85 per cent of school children with ADHD meet the criteria for at least one other diagnosis that falls under the ESSENCE umbrella, while 100 per cent of preschool children with autism meet the criteria for at least one other learning/communication, psychiatric, neurological, or medical disorder diagnosis. Almost all conditions in the ESSENCE group occur more commonly among boys, but many girls are overlooked or misdiagnosed during their early childhood years.

After the overview of these syndromes, 1 will provide three examples of ESSENCE in the form of case descriptions, summarize the lifetime prognosis for ESSENCE, and finally describe the need to organize centres for investigation and treatment.

Chapter 2

ADHD, Inattention, Impulsivity, and Restlessness

History of ADHD

ADHD acquired its current name in 1987 when the *Diagnostic and Statistical Manual of Mental Disorders Third Edition Revised* (DSM-III-R) was published. Up until then, several different words and terms had been used for ADHD, including attention deficits (Melchior Adam Weikard 1775), mental restlessness (Alexander Crichton 1798), "a defect in moral consciousness with incapacity for sustained attention" (George Still 1902), minimal brain damage, minimal brain dysfunction (MBD), hyperkinetic disorder, DAMP (deficits in attention, motor control, and perception), and ADD (attention-deficit disorder).

Diagnostic criteria

The diagnostic criteria for ADHD published in the DSM-III-R (APA 1987) were revised in the DSM-IV (1994). Since then, criteria for the disorder including in the DSM-5 and ICD-11 have remained almost the same (Box 2.1).

Box 2.1 Attention-deficit/hyperactivity disorder according to DSM-5 (symptom criteria generally consistent with ICD-11)

A. Either A1 or A2

A1. Inattention: Six (or more) of the following nine symptoms have persisted for at least six months to a degree that is inconsistent with developmental level and that impacts directly on social and academic/occupational activities:

1. Often fails to give close attention to details or makes careless mistakes in schoolwork, at work, or during other activities.

2. Often has difficulty sustaining attention in tasks or play activities.

3. Often does not seem to listen when spoken to directly.

4. Often does not follow through on instructions and fails to finish schoolwork, chores, or duties in the workplace.

5. Often has difficulty organizing tasks and activities.

6. Often avoids, dislikes, or is reluctant to engage in tasks that require sustained mental effort.

7. Often loses things necessary for tasks or activities.

8. Is often easily distracted by extraneous stimuli (for older adolescents and adults, may include unrelated thoughts).

9. Is often forgetful in daily activities.

A2. Hyperactivity and impulsivity: Six (or more) of the following symptoms have persisted for at least six months to a degree that is inconsistent with developmental level and that impact directly on social and academic/occupational activities:

1. Often fidgets with or taps hands or feet or squirms in seat.

2. Often leaves seat in situations when remaining seated is expected.

3. Often runs about or climbs in situations where it is inappropriate (in adolescents or adults, may be limited to feeling restless).

4. Often unable to play or engage in leisure activities quietly.

5. Is often "on the go", acting as if "driven by a motor".

6. Often talks excessively.

7. Often blurts out an answer before a question has been completed.

8. Often has difficulty waiting his or her turn.

9. Often interrupts or intrudes on others.

B. Several inattentive or hyperactive-impulsive symptoms were present prior to age 12 (age 7 under DSM-5).

C. Criteria for the disorder are met in two or more settings (e.g. at home, school or work, with friends or relatives, or in other activities).

D. There must be clear evidence that the symptoms interfere with or reduce the quality of social, academic, or occupational functioning.

E. The symptoms do not occur exclusively during the course of schizophrenia or another psychotic disorder and are not better accounted for by another mental disorder (e.g. mood disorder, anxiety disorder, dissociative disorder, or a personality disorder).

Specify based on current presentation:

Combined presentation: If both Criterion A1 (Inattention) and Criterion A2 (Hyperactivity-impulsivity) are met for the past six months.

Predominantly inattentive presentation: If Criterion A1 (Inattention) is met but Criterion A2 (Hyperactivity-impulsivity) is not met and three or more symptoms from Criterion A2 have been present for the past six months.

Inattentive presentation (restrictive): If Criterion A1 (Inattention) is met but no more than two symptoms from Criterion A2 (Hyperactivity-impulsivity) have been present for the past six months.

Predominantly hyperactive/impulsive presentation: If Criterion A2 (Hyperactivity-impulsivity) is met and Criterion A1 (Inattention) is not met for the past six months.

Coding note: For individuals (especially adolescents and adults) who currently have symptoms with impairment that no longer meet full criteria, "in partial remission" should be specified.

There are different clinical presentations of ADHD. ADHD, mainly inattentive subtype (sometimes referred to as ADD without the H – attention-deficit disorder), is characterized by six or more symptoms of inattention; ADHD, predominantly hyperactive-impulsive subtype, is characterized by six or more symptoms of hyperactivity/impulsivity; and ADHD, combined subtype, is characterized by six or more symptoms from the inattention group of problems plus six or more symptoms from the hyperactive-impulsive group of problems. There is also a category referred to as ADHD in remission for cases that once met full criteria for the diagnosis, but now no longer do so in spite of still leading to impairment.

"Pure" hyperactivity without any symptoms of inattention (or other "comorbidity") is possibly more of a "personality type" than a disorder, and is rarely associated with any severe functional impairment. ADHD, combined subtype, is nowadays often recognized in the first seven years of life, whereas ADHD, inattentive subtype (ADD), usually is not assessed or diagnosed until beyond 8 years of age or even much later (and particularly late – or even missed altogether in childhood/adolescence – in girls).

Prevalence

Many studies from around the world have shown that 3–7 per cent of all school children meet the diagnostic criteria for ADHD. A relatively much smaller number of studies of adults have shown a corresponding rate of 2–5 per cent. The rate varies depending on exactly which diagnostic criteria have been used and on how impairment has been defined. The vast majority of children who meet full criteria for ADHD in early life will have remaining symptoms and problems in adult life, often into old age, even though the symptoms may not be as many or as obvious, or may seem to fluctuate and become more impairing again in the process of ageing.

Boys are affected more often than girls, but girls and women are often missed, which contributes to a clinical impression of an even more skewed male-to-female ratio. Studies on adults suggest that the real male-to-female ratio is closer to 2:1 than the 3–4:1 often quoted in the literature. Among children whose parents seek professional help before the child's eighth birthday, boys outnumber girls by almost 5:1.

ADHD occurs in all parts of the world and at about the same prevalence rates in all the various countries and regions where epidemiological studies have been performed. ADHD associated with various types of conduct problems and extremes of oppositional behaviours is probably overrepresented in "psychosocial problems" settings.

Causes and risk factors

ADHD is strongly genetic in many cases. Several twin studies have shown heritability rates of 0.70–0.80. Specific genes that have been shown to be associated with ADHD include those that are involved in the formation and metabolism of transmitters and hormones such as dopamine, norepinephrine, glutamate, and melatonin.

Negative influences during the foetal period and the first few years of life increase the risk of ADHD. Such influences include alcohol effects during foetal development, certain intra- and extrauterine infections, extremes of prematurity, seizures in the newborn period (which may be negative in and of themselves, but also a signal that there are already other brain problems present), and various kinds of negative effects of treatments for malignant disorders (chemotherapy, hormones, radiation).

Often there is a combination of genetic and biological environmental negative influences. An adverse psychosocial situation increases the risk of oppositional, aggressive, destructive, and conduct problem behaviours, but the basic problems in ADHD are associated with brain variation/deviation that is not primarily associated with psychosocial environment.

Some parts of the central nervous system are smaller in volume or have unusual functioning in ADHD. This applies particularly to the frontal lobes, basal ganglia, corpus callosum, and the cerebellum (and possibly the brainstem). The reward systems in the brain tend to function at a low level, leading to increased risks for the feeling of boredom and lack of interest (specifically for tasks that require sustained attention), sensation-seeking behaviours, risk taking, and abuse of substances and dependence on other fast-reward behaviours.

Early symptoms

The first symptoms that lead to concern in ADHD may well be related to unusual motor behaviours, extremely early onset of walking independently (occasionally, though, very late onset even after 18 months may occur), inattention (not listening), late onset of spoken language/language disorder, but also sleep problems, emotional dysregulation, impulsivity/hyperactivity, and lack of fear of (obvious) danger.

Extremes of oppositional behaviours, temper tantrums, saying no, and often being negative and aggressive are also very common, and are sometimes separately diagnosed as oppositional defiant disorder (ODD). This added problem increases the risk of later conduct disorder (i.e. behaviours and acts shown by children and youth that had they occurred in adulthood would have been regarded as criminal and would have led to prosecution) and adult antisocial personality disorder. This, in turn, is associated with high rates of impulsive and drug-related crimes, including violent acts during outbursts in affect. It is not clear whether or not ODD should be seen as a completely separate neurodevelopmental category under the ESSENCE umbrella or if it should rather be seen as a temperamental or personality trait or as a severity measure for the underlying neurodevelopmental problem (e.g. ADHD).

Motor coordination problems (such as in DCD) and language problem/communication disorder in ADHD instead signal an extremely increased risk for school and academic problems, and later failures in workplaces followed by unemployment and, later, sick leave and early retirement (Rasmussen & Gillberg 2000). In the group with ADHD, DCD, and language disorder, the clinical presentation is often one of attention deficits, passivity, "daydreaming", and hypo- rather than hyperactivity (the type of problems still often referred to as ADD) (Kadesjö *et al.* 2001).

Symptoms during the early school years

ADHD often shows its true colours only during the first school years. The inability to sit still, "ants in the pants", difficulties concentrating, a tendency to get bored quickly, distractibility, and a habit of always talking too much and too loud and too impulsively with no in-built stop-it warning are things that become more and more disrupting and annoying to people in the immediate environment, at a time when sitting still and concentrating are things that are considered crucial for learning and development.

Impulse control problems and short-fuse behaviours and tantrums in connection with demands are very frequent. In fact, the inability to control temper and changes from "sunny" to "meltdown" within seconds are among the most frequent of all symptoms in children and adults with ADHD, even though such problems are not among the current diagnostic criteria for ADHD. Perseverance failure is almost the rule. Some children are extremely overactive (mostly boys, but some girls too) and impulsive; others (more girls, but boys too) are more "dreaming", "in their own little bubble or world", or "just not there". There is a large subgroup of cases of ADHD with an almost narcoleptic tendency to fall asleep or at least "nod off" from time to time. Some school-age children with ADHD fluctuate between the two hyper- and hypoactive extremes and are likely to be diagnosed with ADHD combined presentation.

Girls with ADHD, much like girls in the general population, are – on average – less motorically (hyper-) active than boys. This is one of the major reasons why ADHD in girls is often not even considered when it comes to diagnostic assessments for depression, anxiety, eating disorders (including obesity), and self-harm. Of course, there are girls who are extremely hyperactive, but the high activity level more often shows as extremes of garrulousness, inability to keep quiet, and a constant movement of fingers and hands and touching of own face or hair, rather than the running-around activities shown by so many of the boys with ADHD (Kopp 2010).

Symptoms during late adolescence and adulthood

Many individuals with ADHD become less obviously "hyperactive" with age. What remains is usually a feeling of inner hyperactivity, restlessness, nervosity, and an overall, almost overwhelming quality of being stressed, under stress, or "stressed out". Many young people and adults who show up in clinics for such problems are considered – usually without any attempt to enquire about or diagnose ADHD – anxious, exhausted, or "burned out". Unfortunately, still, many adult psychiatrists and general practitioners have too little knowledge or experience when it comes to ADHD, so that in such cases diagnoses of generalized anxiety disorder (GAD) or depression will be made instead of the real underlying problem of ADHD. This is particularly unhelpful, given that the evidence-based treatment for ADHD is almost the opposite of what is often offered for GAD and depression.

Attention deficits, concentration difficulties, and difficulties with time concepts, planning, and organizing remain in almost all throughout life. Extremes of talkativeness and, conversely, problems with quickly joining a conversation can lead to problems in social interaction settings. Others still can have problems when relating what has happened or when telling a story so that they can be perceived as very circumstantial and "boring".

Many adult people with ADHD (usually undiagnosed in childhood) attend health services of various kinds for problems related to chronic pain and fibromyalgia. Sleep problems (insomnia, early awakening, reduced or increased sleep need, disrupted sleep cycle) are the rule in the whole group (even though there are those who consider their clearly abnormal sleep behaviour "just right"). There is a much increased rate of hypersomnias in ADHD (including the extreme referred to as narcolepsy).

Individuals with other chronic problems and illnesses (diabetes, cerebral palsy (CP), epilepsy, bowel problems, asthma, obesity) and concurrent ADHD are often considered "difficult to treat" or "unmotivated". If their concomitant ADHD is recognized and treated, their "major" illness (diabetes, epilepsy, obesity, etc.) often becomes much more "manageable". There is growing evidence that individuals with ADHD are at much increased risk of later eating disorders, possibly related to high levels of impulsivity. Both obesity and bulimic behaviours/bulimia nervosa occur at high or very high rates in the life trajectories of people with ADHD.

There are also studies suggesting a strong link between so-called minor cognitive impairment (MCI) in older age on the one hand and ADHD on the other. Working memory problems are often at the core of the ADHD syndrome and with (older age) related ("normal") memory problems added in (after about 60 years of age), the impression of a "major" memory problem can become striking, leading to consultation at memory clinics or referrals for Alzheimer's disease. In such cases, a diagnosis of MCI is often made (on the basis of recorded problems with short time/working memory), and the patient is scheduled for re-testing/follow-up within a year or two. At retest, results are usually at the exact same level as a year or two ago, showing that there is no decline or dementia. In such cases, it will be very helpful to take a good childhood/lifetime history of ADHD problems, and often to make an appropriate diagnosis of ADHD, and even to try relevant treatment for ADHD at this late stage in life.

Cognitive function and profile

On cognitive tests (including so-called IQ tests) children and adults with ADHD can show results that range from intellectual disability to extremely above-average results. In about half of all cases, the so-called profile is often uneven, with poor results on subtests that measure attention, speed, working memory, and motor performance. The other half very often have a generally "even" low level, and many of these fall within the category of "learning problems" or "borderline intellectual functioning" (BIF). The BIF diagnosis has recently fallen out of fashion, and some children who are now diagnosed as suffering from ADHD (and, of course, they do in the sense that they meet the symptom criteria for ADHD) actually "only" have BIF, sometimes very close to and overlapping the level of intellectual disability.

Interventions and treatments

There are many effective interventions and treatments for ADHD, even though there is currently no cure. Psychoeducation about ADHD and its related ESSENCE for individuals and families (including the explicitly detailed diagnosis itself and information about what those details mean in the individual case) is essential and should be regarded as a treatment/intervention in and of itself, and not be seen as just delivering a label. Individually tailored education plans, computerized working memory training, non-aggressive/non-violent martial arts, physical exercise, and yoga have all been reported to have some beneficial effects regarding ADHD symptoms, but long-term effects have not been demonstrated and there is clearly a need for more research into all of the said interventions.

There is very good evidence that ADHD medication with stimulants or noradrenergic reuptake inhibitors has good effects in reducing ADHD symptoms and, in the case of stimulants, long-term positive effects include reduction of crime rates, drug abuse, and road traffic accidents. Some studies indicate moderately positive effects of Omega-3 supplementation, both with regard to attention abilities and reading skills (Johnson *et al.* 2009;

Johnson *et al.* 2017). Recently, a randomized controlled study of PR-ESSENCE (Proactive Resolutions for children with ESSENCE) has shown very positive effects on family functioning and global child functioning while not necessarily dramatically decreasing the level of ADHD symptomatology. PR-ESSENCE is a sort of conjoint family intervention where the child's cognitive functions are in focus and parents and children together get to solve everyday ESSENCE behaviour and other problems during 6–10 sessions separated by about two weeks (Johnson *et al.* 2020).

In the vast majority of cases with ADHD, a combination of interventions, often combined with stimulant medication, is needed to obtain optimal results. It is also always necessary to put ADHD in the ESSENCE perspective and be aware that a host of other ("non-ADHD") ESSENCE problems and symptoms are usually present and these (e.g. DCD, dyslexia, learning problems of other kinds, speech and language disorder, ODD, autistic features, and obsessive-compulsive disorder) will often require separate interventions.

Outcome

ADHD should usually be seen as a lifelong neurodiversity variant or neurodevelopmental disorder. This applies even in cases where the most obvious "external" symptoms gradually abate and even seem to disappear. "On the inside" of such individuals with childhood ADHD, there usually remains into adulthood (even into old age) a sense of inner restlessness, attention difficulties, working memory problems, and executive function deficits including difficulties planning ahead, organizing work, and "sticking it out". As has already been mentioned, there are many psychiatric and psychosocial comorbid problems that may emerge over a lifetime (including depression, anxiety, chronic pain, chronic fatigue, obesity and other eating disorders, drug abuse, and drug-related criminal activities). Mortality is much increased. Early intervention will help reduce these poor outcomes and many of those who get good early help can have good, even excellent outcomes (in the face of still having some of the basic ADHD symptoms left, symptoms that might not be obvious at casual observation or assessment). Without such early intervention, the naturalistic outcome of ADHD is poor or very poor in at least half of all cases with onset in early childhood. Unless picked up and intervened for in childhood, ADHD will remain one of the greatest public health problems/threats in modern societies. However, if recognized, assessed, and "treated", it can also be a diagnosis that can inspire hope and determination to avoid the poor outcomes associated with gang identity, drug abuse, and reckless driving.

Chapter 3

Autism

History of autism

Autism has very likely been around for thousands of years, even though it has not always been referred to as such. Prominent autism researcher Uta Frith (Frith 2003) has drawn on historical accounts to provide a particularly early example: brother Juniper, a 13th-century monk and disciple of Francis of Assisi, corresponds perfectly with our current idea of "typical" autism. Around the end of the 18th century and beginning of the 19th century, there were cases of "feral children" presumed to have been "raised" by woodland animals. Today, their behaviour would certainly have been classified as typical autism. Jean Itard wrote in detail about one of these children, the wild boy from Aveyron. In 1908, Theodor Heller described cases of "infantile dementia" that would probably be considered "regressive autism" today. In the 1920s, Eva Ssuchareva reported on so-called schizoid children – today, they would likely have been diagnosed with autism or Asperger's syndrome. In the 1930s, Hans Asperger began to describe what he called "autistic psychopathy/personality disorder" (Asperger 1944). Leo Kanner coined the term "early infantile autism" in 1943 (Kanner 1943), presumably after one of Asperger's students brought his attention to the phenomenon.

Today, we consider the defining features of autism to be early-onset severe abnormalities in terms of mutual social/communicative interaction and concurrent behavioural disorders marked by stereotypical movements and speech, along with general mental rigidity.

Prevalence

Around 1 per cent of school-age children and an almost equal proportion of adults have autism. There used to be clear distinctions between different kinds of autism – autistic syndrome, Asperger's syndrome, disintegrative disorder, other autistic-like conditions – but in current diagnostic manuals, all of these conditions fall under the same umbrella, namely "autism spectrum disorder". This term is problematic in that autism is not one spectrum with a shared root cause, and it also cannot be considered a disorder of something that was once "normal" (on the contrary, the condition is typically present all the way from birth onward) (Waterhouse, London, & Gillberg 2017).

Most cases of classic autism (autistic syndrome) can today be identified and diagnosed before the age of 3, but what is (still) described as Asperger's syndrome often goes (partially) unrecognized until the first years of school.

In practice, typical autism symptoms are still often diagnosed as autism when combined with some degree of general intellectual disability (below the scope of normal IQ) and Asperger's syndrome when combined with normal or high intelligence. Many argue for the utility of Asperger's syndrome as a separate diagnosis, due to its perception as less severe than autism and its frequent association with relatively high general intellectual ability.

Diagnostic criteria

The first published diagnostic criteria for autism came in the 1960s in the form of a checklist of typical symptoms (designed by Mildred Creak). Operationalized criteria for infantile autism were established in 1980 in DSM-III. These criteria were further detailed in 1987 with the publication of DSM-III-R, only to be revised yet again in 1994 in DSM-IV. The latest revision was made in 2013 in the DSM-5.

Diagnostic criteria for Asperger's syndrome were not published until the late 1980s (Gillberg & Gillberg 1989) (Box 3.1).

In recent years the rate of "registered" autism has increased dramatically, even to the extent that overdiagnosis has been discussed. However, it seems clear that "typical" autism is no more common now than 20 years ago and that many children with ESSENCE receive autism diagnoses even when they only have some/a few autistic symptoms (Arvidsson *et al.* 2018).

Box 3.1 Autism spectrum disorder criteria according to DSM-5

A. Persistent deficits in social communication and social interaction across multiple contexts, as manifested by the following, currently or by history; examples are illustrative, not exhaustive (see text):

1. Deficits in social-emotional reciprocity, ranging, for example, from abnormal social approach and failure of normal back-and-forth conversation; to reduced sharing of interests, emotions, or affect; to failure to initiate or respond to social interactions.

2. Deficits in nonverbal communicative behaviours used for social interaction, ranging, for example, from poorly integrated verbal and nonverbal communication; to abnormalities in eye contact and body language or deficits in understanding and use of gestures; to a total lack of facial expressions and nonverbal communication.

3. Deficits in developing, maintaining, and understanding relationships, ranging, for example, from difficulties adjusting behaviour to suit various social contexts; to difficulties in sharing imaginative play or in making friends; to absence of interest in peers.

Specify current severity:

Severity is based on social communication impairments and restricted, repetitive patterns of behaviour.

B. Restricted, repetitive patterns of behaviour, interests, or activities, as manifested by at least two of the following, currently or by history; examples are illustrative, not exhaustive (see text):

1. Stereotyped or repetitive motor movements, use of objects, or speech.

2. Insistence on sameness, inflexible adherence to routines, or ritualized patterns of verbal or nonverbal behaviour.

3. Highly restricted, fixated interests that are abnormal in intensity or focus.

4. Hyper- or hyporeactivity to sensory input or unusual interest in sensory aspects of the environment.

Specify current severity:

Severity is based on social communication impairments and restricted, repetitive patterns of behaviour.

C. Symptoms must be present in the early developmental period (but may not become fully manifest until social demands exceed limited capacities, or may be masked by learned strategies in later life).

D. Symptoms cause clinically significant impairment in social, occupational, or other important areas of current functioning.

E. These disturbances are not better explained by intellectual disability or global developmental delay. Intellectual disability and autism spectrum disorder frequently co-occur; to make comorbid diagnoses of autism spectrum disorder and intellectual disability, social communication should be below that expected for general developmental level.

Note: Individuals with a well-established DSM-IV diagnosis of autistic disorder, Asperger's syndrome, or pervasive developmental disorder not otherwise specified should be given the diagnosis of autism spectrum disorder. Individuals who have marked deficits in social communication, but whose symptoms do not otherwise meet the criteria for autism spectrum disorder, should be evaluated for social (pragmatic) communication disorder.

Specify if:

With or without accompanying intellectual impairment.

With or without accompanying language impairment.

Associated with a known medical or genetic condition or environmental factor.

Associated with another neurodevelopmental, mental, or behavioural disorder.

With catatonia.

Cognitive profile

Neuropsychological test results might indicate anything from severe intellectual disability to exceptional intelligence in individuals with autism. The cognitive profile is virtually always uneven – that is, characterized by clear strengths and weaknesses. General intellectual ability and especially verbal ability might be very poor, and in such cases the clinical presentation tends to align most closely with "classic autism". Conversely, if general intellectual ability is – relatively speaking – very high, the clinical impression usually aligns with Asperger's syndrome. Around 1 in 5 or 6 people with autism (Asperger's syndrome included) has intellectual disability as well.

Early symptoms

There are many possible first symptoms of autism: motor abnormalities, abnormal perception (unexpected/strange reactions to sound, light, smell, taste, touch, pain, cold, heat), inattention, low interest in initiating social interaction (including absence of pointing), rigid demands for rituals and strong opposition to change, tantrums in response to any adversity, stereotypical movements (such as hand-waving or head-bobbing), delayed speech, sleep disorders, unstable mood, impulsiveness/hyperactivity, and a poor sense of what constitutes real danger.

Many of these symptoms are also typical of ADHD, which makes differential diagnosis difficult or even impossible at an early age. Childhood autism is a near-perfect predictor of adult autism (almost 100% of individuals diagnosed with autism before the age of 10 also meet criteria after the age of 20), while 85 per cent of children with Asperger's syndrome meet diagnostic criteria for autism ten years later; the rest have autistic symptoms without reaching the diagnostic threshold.

Autism is almost always associated with other problems: intellectual disability, motor disorder, language disorder, ADHD, tics, epilepsy, and a range of other neurological and medical conditions.

Autism is much more common among boys than girls, but the diagnosis also tends to go undetected in girls throughout preschool (girls are generally more "social" than boys, so the possibility of autism is rarely even raised), creating the impression of an exceedingly skewed gender distribution. Girls diagnosed with autism before entering school are often just as severely impaired as boys with the same diagnosis, but the vast majority of girls with typical autism are not detected and diagnosed until later in life. If there were better biological or neuropsychological markers for autism, the gender ratio would likely even out significantly.

Symptoms later in life

The core symptoms of autism rarely change dramatically over time. Most adults who met diagnostic criteria as children continue to struggle with social interaction and rapid communication with other people. They have a tendency to grow obsessive and compulsive, particularly in stress-filled situations.

Virtually all children who meet diagnostic criteria for autism struggle with additional difficulties and problems, but it should be noted that many of these – such as ADHD, dyslexia, and depression – are much more readily treatable than the autism itself. For example, ADHD medication can have very positive effects even when autism is the core diagnosis. Many adults with autism should therefore be re-evaluated with a stronger focus on other ESSENCE problems.

Causes and risk factors

Autism, like ADHD, is very strongly influenced by genes, and several twin studies have indicated that heritability ranges from 70 to over 90 per cent (Lundström *et al.* 2012). Many of the mutated genes or "variant genes" found to be correlated with autism influence formation, function, and diffusion of synapses in the brain. Other important genes affect the brain's "scaffolding" – that is, the system that enables nerve fibres to find the right partner to pair with. Additional genetic abnormalities have been established in the melatonin system, which partially controls our circadian rhythm and sleep pattern, and the contactin system, which we need in order to form auditory pathways; damage to this system manifests as auditory perception disorders (Jamain *et al.* 2003; Delorme *et al.* 2013; see section above on early symptoms).

Many studies on autism have produced results suggesting that the condition is only rarely – if ever – caused by a single abnormal gene. In most cases, two or more genetic abnormalities combine (potentially along with various environmental factors) to form the clinical symptomatology that we call autism.

In some cases, one might also develop/have autism without genetic factors playing any specific part in the condition's development.

Adverse influences during the foetal period and the first years of life increase the risk of autism. These include effects of alcohol and medication during pregnancy, extremely premature birth, neonatal seizures, and brain infections occurring in the first years of life. Many cases can be traced back to a combination of genetic factors and negative environmental influences. Some conditions – including fragile X syndrome, tuberous sclerosis, neurofibromatosis, Möbius syndrome – can cause autism "on their own".

Interventions and treatments

Autism can almost never be "cured", except in rare cases when the diagnosis is directly caused by an underlying treatable disease (e.g. phenylketonuria (PKU), mitochondrial diseases, and tuberous sclerosis).

Early psychoeducational measures are likely of great value in improving families' quality of life, and intervention programmes centred on special education and behavioural therapy can prove very effective in reducing behavioural disorders and communication difficulties, but it is still unclear what the isolated impact of these programmes is on lifetime prognosis (Fernell *et al.* 2011).

As of yet, there is no medication with proven effectiveness in terms of specifically treating autistic symptoms. However, several studies have suggested that oxytocin might alleviate the difficulties in social interaction (not yet in general clinical use for this purpose) and that melatonin can help to address the sleep difficulties that people with autism often face.

Bumetanide, a diuretic that has long been used to treat heart disease in both children and adults, has in recent years turned out to be effective in reducing autistic symptoms. Bumetanide "normalizes" the gamma aminobutyric acid (GABA)/glutamate balance in the brain, a balance that is often "abnormal" in individuals with autism and other neuropsychiatric disorders. However, this substance has not yet been approved for the treatment of autism.

ADHD in autism should be treated in the same manner whether it occurs in conjunction with autism or not. The same mostly goes for epilepsy, although one must be aware that certain anti-epileptic drugs (mainly benzodiazepines) might exacerbate the autistic symptoms.

Outcome

Associated problems have a greater bearing on prognosis than the number of autistic symptoms per se. Autism predicts autism, but not necessarily a poor psychosocial outcome. If there are no severe "comorbidities" (e.g. intellectual disability, language disorder, or ADHD), it is entirely possible to lead an independent and fulfilling adult life (Helles 2016).

A very small group of people with autism end up committing extreme crimes – crimes that might have been prevented with early accurate diagnosis and psychoeducational measures. That being said, the vast majority are, if anything, more law-abiding than other people.

Chapter 4

Developmental Coordination Disorder (DCD)

History of DCD

Moderate (and, of course, major) problems with gross and fine motor function or with the coordination of movements can lead to considerable functional impairment in everyday-life situations. Children who are perceived as "late" (which is often equivalent to deviant) in their gross or fine motor development have long been described as clumsy, klutzes, or merely "awkward". The clumsy child syndrome, dyspraxia, and motor-perceptual handicap all came into common parlance in the early 1970s. From the late 1980s, these "clumsy" or "ill-coordinated" children received their own generally accepted diagnostic category of DCD (developmental coordination disorder) in the DSM-III-R (APA 1987). Not being able to learn how to ride a bike, swim, skate, or ski, or to participate in group games at a rate similar to age peers leads to a sense of inadequacy and "not belonging", to social exclusion, and often to anxiety and depression. DCD remains one of the most often neglected ESSENCE problem groups, and many clinicians fail to make an appropriate diagnosis, hence blocking pathways to effective interventions. Children with ADHD and/or autism very often also have DCD, but the motor coordination problems are somehow perceived as inherent in the other diagnoses and are very often neither recognized nor diagnosed, and much less intervened for. There is a great need for more focus on DCD, both in clinical practice and research.

Diagnostic criteria

The diagnostic criteria for DCD in the DSM-5 are rather vague. In clinical practice, the diagnosis is made in a young person who is clumsy, manually or with regard to gross motor function, and whose overall movements are ill-coordinated. In addition, the motor examination reveals a number of different signs, including difficulties with hand pro-supination (dysdiadochokiniesis), balance (such as when standing on one foot), a deviant pattern of associated movements (e.g. when walking on the lateral aspects of the feet), or "hard neurological signs" (including abnormal reflexes, mild spasticity, or extreme hypotonia). The diagnosis of DCD is only made when the individual has personal suffering or is negatively affected in terms of adaptive daily-life functioning.

Prevalence

Several different studies have demonstrated that DCD is one of the most common problem types in the group of ESSENCE. About 5 per cent of all children meet the criteria for the disorder at early school ages (Kadesjö & Gillberg 1999). It appears that boys outnumber girls by at least a ratio of 2:1 (meaning that about 7% of boys and 3% of girls are affected). DCD symptoms remain in the majority for years and even decades, even though the full criteria for the DSM-5 diagnostic category may no longer be met in adulthood.

Symptoms

The DCD motor problems more often than not are associated with visuo-perceptual problems of various kinds. Auditory perceptual difficulties and sensory over- and under-sensitivity are also quite commonly associated problems. A very large proportion of all with DCD have marked autistic features (and vice versa).

DCD occurs in about half of all individuals with ADHD, almost all of those who meet criteria for Asperger's syndrome, and half of those with speech and language disorder (and at about the same rate in those with dyslexia), and is prevalent in virtually all the syndromes that fall under the ESSENCE umbrella. It is possible that Tourette's syndrome may be unassociated with DCD; in most such cases, apart from the tics, motor performance is "normal" or even above average. DCD carries a very high risk of associated anxiety and depression, perhaps particularly in boys who tend to be bullied even more than girls if they cannot contribute in sports teams and look awkward and ungainly in their movements. Anxiety and depression in DCD are often even more apparent in those with marked autistic features. In exceptional cases, the DCD might be the child's/adolescent's only problem, but the vast majority have a combination of other ESSENCE problems alongside their motor difficulties.

DCD is very often associated with late onset of walking unsupported (after 14 months of age), and an overall impression of "motor cautiousness" in the toddler years. Mild to moderate (indeed, even occasionally very marked) muscular hypotonus (low muscle tone) is typical of many. In a smaller group, muscle tone may instead be high and bordering on hypertonus and "spasticity". Smaller still is the group who later meet criteria for DCD who bottom-shuffled their way across the floor from maybe 10 to 18 months and then started to walk unsupported. Some children with DCD do not "crawl" like other children (and there is no evidence that starting to learn to crawl in adult life will benefit those with DCD in childhood who never crawled as babies/toddlers).

The first visible symptoms of DCD – apart from "late development" – can be very varied. Unusual/"flat" facial expressions with little facial movement, dissociated developmental rate in upper and lower body (faster or slower in arms compared with legs), imprecise and fidgety/jerky movements, late-developing pincer grip, and late-developing finger pointing are common first indicators. Overall muscular hypotonia may become most obvious around 18–36 months when the child may sit like a haybag and have clear difficulties straightening the back.

From about age 3–4 years, it becomes more and more obvious that the child is "clumsy" and ill-coordinated in movements, and has difficulties eating with a spoon, knife, and fork, using a crayon or a pencil, dressing and undressing, putting on and taking off shoes, learning to ride on a tricycle, catching a ball (even a big one), or participating in simple motor imitation games (e.g. itsy-bitsy spider).

From about age 5–6 years, it becomes more specifically obvious that the child is clumsy, and has difficulties with most things "motor". Standing on one foot, jumping up and down on one foot, riding a bicycle, keeping balance, walking with a straight back, skiing, skating, participating in ball games, eating and drinking without spilling, writing and drawing, holding on to a pencil, brushing teeth – all these things that other children do not think about but "just do" – are difficult, maybe even impossible. It is also common for oral-motor problems to make life difficult, with speech being affected, slurred, or slowed, and swallowing problems leading to choking behaviour. The prevalence of enuresis and encopresis is also much higher in DCD than in non-DCD.

Causes and risk factors

The underlying causes and risk factors in DCD are partly associated with genetic factors; parents and siblings very often have (or have had in the past) similar problems. There is also a considerable "co-genetic" link with ADHD, autism, and speech and language disorder, as demonstrated in those many extended families where there is an increased rate of different combinations of all of these syndromes, disorders, and problems. In some cases of DCD there is a link with pre- and perinatal risk factors that are known to be associated with brain damage, such as extremes of prematurity and intrapartal or neonatal asphyxiation.

Interventions and treatments

There are now well-validated interventions and treatments for DCD with task-oriented training (including weight and treadmill training) programmes of different types. The best solutions are not always the inclusion of the child in large groups of other children (such as in physical education (PE) at school or ball games); such approaches often lead to feelings of shame, anger, and of being "stupid and ugly", and can lead to outright bullying.

It is important for children who are "clumsy" and ill-coordinated to have their difficulties recognized and acknowledged, and for families and teachers to have the problems "named". Understanding that the child is who he/she is and not somebody who is lazy or "unwilling to try" is crucially important for his/her self-esteem and overall positive development. Many young people with DCD who are depressed, listless, isolated among their peers, and outright bullied can come out of their feelings of hopelessness if people around them own up to the fact that there is a real problem, that the child cannot help that he/she will fail in all sorts of everyday-life situations (in PE, sports, ball games, dancing, at mealtimes, in situations requiring quick dressing and undressing), and that the problems cannot be solved by the child just "shaping up", "putting in an effort", or "exercising more". Focused task-training programmes aimed at improving the specific skills required for eating with a spoon, drinking from a cup, tying shoelaces, putting a T-shirt on, catching a ball, holding a pencil, and typing and hitting the right buttons are well validated and should be used in all cases (Polatajko & Cantin 2005). Such training should be performed in individual or small group sessions, not in front of a large group of other children. Stimulant medication can also be helpful in improving fine motor skills in the group with DCD who have comorbid ADHD.

Outcome

A small number of individuals with DCD diagnosed in childhood will eventually "grow out" of their coordination difficulties. In the vast majority of cases, some "clumsiness", motor awkwardness, and fumbly behaviours will remain throughout adult life. However this does not mean that mental health outcome is generally poor. Many of the associated childhood problems can be positively affected through early interventions. The link between childhood DCD and depression/anxiety needs to be recognized by health professionals.

It is highly likely that depressed mood and anxiety problems can be mitigated through psychoeducation and task training in cases with underlying DCD.

Chapter 5

Speech and Language Disorders

This short chapter could very well have been the longest in the book. However, delving into this area in detail would require a very thorough account of literature spanning several centuries, which simply would not be possible in this context.

Motor abnormalities are perhaps the very earliest signs that the child will eventually turn out to have severe neurodevelopmental or psychiatric problems. However, there is a much clearer, more evidence-based link between early abnormalities in speech development and childhood ESSENCE problems.

There is no doubt that speech screening at around 2.5 years of age is the surest and most effective way of finding as many children as possible with significantly increased risk of presenting with ESSENCE conditions when followed up several years later. Two-and-a-half-year-old children who (1) cannot say 50 words, or (2) cannot understand simple verbal instructions, or (3) have such difficulties articulating that people outside their closest family cannot understand them, very often have ESSENCE. Early school-age follow-ups show that two-thirds or more have severe ESSENCE problems beyond just speech difficulties, and that virtually all the rest have lingering speech problems or dyslexic difficulties.

Prevalence

Many countries have estimated the prevalence of speech and language disorders among preschool-age children (2.5–6 years) at around 4 to 5 per cent. Boys are affected much more often than girls. The idea of "specific" language disorder among children used to be quite widespread, but over the last few decades research has shown that language disorder (not caused by lack of language stimulation) is usually associated with a host of other ESSENCE problems, thus meaning that the language disorder is not "specific" at all. Isolated speech and language delay is extremely rare, but it does occur in certain families.

Box 5.1 Speech and language disorders
Speech sound disorder

A. Persistent problems with speech sound production that interferes with speech intelligibility or prevents verbal communication of messages.

B. Disturbance causes limitations in effective communication that interfere with social, academic, or occupational functioning, individually or in combination.

C. Onset is in the early developmental period.

D. Not attributable to congenital or acquired conditions, such as cerebral palsy, cleft palate, deafness or hearing loss, traumatic brain injury, or other medical or neurological problem/disorders.

Language disorder

A. Persistent problems in the acquisition and use of language across modalities (i.e. spoken, written, sign language, or other) due to deficits in comprehension or production that include the following:

   1. Limited vocabulary.

   2. Limited sentence structure.

---

3. Impairments in discourse.

B. Language abilities are substantially and quantifiably below those expected for age, resulting in functional limitations in effective communication, social, academic, or occupational functioning, individually or in combination.

C. Onset is in the early developmental period.

D. Problems are not attributable to hearing or other sensory impairment, motor dysfunction, or another medical or neurological condition, and are not better explained by intellectual disability.

Childhood-onset fluency disorder (stuttering)
A. Problems with normal fluency and time patterning of speech that are inappropriate for the individual's age and language level, persist over time, and are characterized by frequent and marked occurrences of one or more of the following:

1. Sound and syllable repetitions.

2. Sound prolongations of consonants as well as vowels.

3. Broken words.

4. Audible or silent blocking.

5. Circumlocutions (word substitutions to avoid problematic words).

6. Problems with words produced with an excess of physical tension.

7. Problems with monosyllabic whole-word repetitions.

B. Cause: anxiety about speaking or limitations in effective communication, social, academic, or occupational functioning, individually or in combination.

C. Onset of symptoms is in the early developmental period.

D. Problems not attributable to a speech-motor or sensory deficit, dysfluency associated with neurological insult, or another medical disorder and is not better explained by another mental disorder.

Social (pragmatic) communication disorder

A. Persistent problems in the social use of verbal and nonverbal communication as manifested by all of the following:

1. Deficits in using communication for social purposes, such as greeting and sharing information, in a manner that is appropriate for the social context.

2. Impairment of the ability to change communication to match context or the needs of the listener, such as speaking differently in a classroom than on a playground, talking differently to a child than to an adult, and avoiding use of overly formal language.

3. Difficulties following rules for conversation and storytelling, such as taking turns in conversation, rephrasing when misunderstood, and knowing how to use verbal and nonverbal signals to regulate interaction.

4. Difficulties understanding what is not explicitly stated and nonliteral or ambiguous meanings of language.

B. Problems result in functional limitations in effective communication, social, academic problems, or occupational functioning, individually or in combination.

C. Onset of problems is in the early developmental period (but deficits may not become fully manifest until social communication demands exceed limited capacities).

D. Problems are not attributable to another medical or neurological disorder or to low abilities in the domains of word structure and grammar, and are not better explained by autism, intellectual disability, global delay, or another mental disorder.

Symptoms

Children with language disorder might have difficulties in phonology (language sounds) and articulation, grammar, semantics (understanding what words mean), and/or pragmatics (use of language for communication). The more areas affected, the more severe and impairing the disorder tends to be. Even so, there are children with isolated abnormalities in only one area where the disorder is very severe.

Common symptoms of language disorder include delayed development of expressive speech (the ability to express oneself), unclear speech, difficulties understanding spoken language, small vocabulary, poor narration ability, repetition/hesitation (including stuttering – see below), and impaired ability to communicate with speech (including muteness).

Pragmatic difficulties (i.e. difficulties communicating) are typical of autism. Many children with language disorder who do not fully meet the criteria for autism have major pragmatic problems. Speech and language pathologists sometimes diagnose these children with semantic-pragmatic language disorder or social communication disorder. The latter diagnosis requires more or less the same symptoms of social-communicative difficulties as autism does. It is confusing, especially to many parents, that such symptoms are categorized as a language disorder and not as an autism-related condition.

Preschool children with severe language disorder often have difficulties that persist throughout the first years of school, although these might change over time. For example, problems with pronunciation and syntax might eventually transition into various kinds of reading and writing difficulties.

Three out of four children with delayed speech development will show symptoms of other ESSENCE problems at school age. This often manifests as a combination of DCD, dyslexia, and ADHD, with or without pronounced autistic traits (a symptom constellation known for several decades in the Nordic countries as Deficits in Attention Motor control and Perception/DAMP).

Stuttering is primarily a speech disorder characterized by involuntary repetitions (jerky, choppy speech), extensions ("mmm", "uhhh"), and interruptions in normal speech flow. People who stutter also often adopt behaviours aimed at moving their speech along or simply avoiding situations that require speaking. Many are afraid to speak and use a variety of strategies to avoid it – everything from avoiding single words to speech situations. Small children are rarely emotionally affected by their stuttering behaviour, but as children approach their teens, many begin to worry or even feel ashamed about their condition.

Some people with Tourette's syndrome (see Chapter 8) have an almost compulsive form of stuttering with "jerky" repetitions and choppy speech.

Stuttering (lasting a few months or more) occurs in at least 1 in 20 children and 1 in 40 adults. It is considered to be significantly more common among males, but certain studies indicate that females are better at hiding their stuttering, making them less likely to be diagnosed.

Causes and risk factors

Language disorder and/or other ESSENCE problems are very often associated with genetic factors in children with speech delay. The combination of genetic factors and limited language stimulation (e.g. because parents and siblings barely speak to the child) is not entirely uncommon. As in other ESSENCE cases, specific brain injuries during pregnancy, delivery, or the first years of life can lead to severe language disorders. Genetic syndromes such as 22q11 deletion syndrome (see Chapter 13) can in some cases also be the root cause.

Interventions and treatments

The intervention programme should primarily consist of examination followed by information about the results, educational adjustments, and speech-language pathology treatment. As in other

ESSENCE cases, the examination must not be limited to just speech and language. Addressing the comorbidity is often the most crucial aspect when treating speech and language disorders (Miniscalco 2007). There are specific speech-language pathology treatment methods for stuttering.

Outcome

Looking at the speech and language disorders in isolation, the prognosis is extremely variable. Usually, some symptoms persist for many years or even throughout life. The problems might appear to have passed by the time the child enters school, but in fact there are usually lingering limitations in vocabulary, phonological difficulties, articulation difficulties, and reading and writing difficulties. Many are eventually diagnosed with dyslexia, sometimes even in adulthood.

Stuttering rarely disappears completely, but with the right treatment in childhood, the perceived disorder can be minimal. However, when severe stuttering problems persist into adulthood, it can be a significant source of silent suffering.

Chapter 6

Intellectual Disability and Learning Problems

The words used to describe or talk about the phenomenon of intellectual disability (ID) have changed many times over the past 200 years. Even over the past few decades, official terminology has changed several times, which means that current and past terminologies do not even overlap. The term "mental retardation" was the most used term up until 2013 when the DSM-5 replaced it with ID. ID is almost always associated with ESSENCE, major brain dysfunction, or severe physical, neurological, and/or psychiatric disorders of various kinds.

History of IQ testing

Intelligence testing (IQ testing) was introduced by Alfred Binet and Théodore Simon in France in 1905. The purpose of such IQ tests (IQ = intelligence quotient) was to assess the child's cognitive ("intellectual" intelligence) abilities, so that appropriate educational stimulation might be provided in schools. Lewis Terman and Maud Merrill developed their own tests on the basis of Binet's original schedules in the 1930s. In the late 1930s and throughout the 1940s, David Wechsler developed the WISC (Wechsler Intelligence Scale for Children) and the WAIS (Wechsler Adult Intelligence Scale), and in the 1960s he published the WPPSI (Wechsler Preschool and Primary Scale of Intelligence). The Wechsler scales have since become the most widely used IQ tests internationally and are regularly re-standardized throughout most of the Western world (Wechsler 2008, 2012, 2014).

There are also "developmental" scales (or DQ tests) used with young children to estimate the developmental (as contrasted with the chronological) age of the child. Nowadays, some of the most often used scales are those developed by Ruth Griffiths and Nancy Bayley.

IQ tests are construed in such a way that the mean value in the general population is 100 and so that about two-thirds of that population have values in the range of 85–115 (which is referred to as "normal" or "average"). If IQ is in the range 70–84, accepted terms are "borderline intellectual functioning" (BIF) or "below average intelligence" or "non-specific learning problems". If IQ is below 70, the now accepted term is "intellectual disability" (ID).

The best and most widely used IQ tests, versions of which have now existed for more than 75 years (e.g. the WISC and the WAIS), are really "neuropsychological tests" in the sense that they include a range of different subtests covering verbal and nonverbal neuropsychological functions that can be looked at and interpreted individually. The various subtests can then be combined to produce overall IQ, verbal and nonverbal IQ, and a number of different IQ "domain" scores.

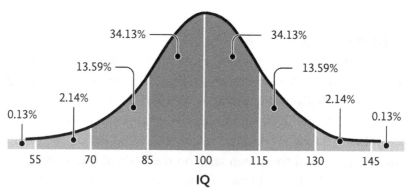

Figure 6.1 *The curve of "normal distribution"*

Intellectual disability (ID) is the term used when making the diagnosis in cases with the combination of tested IQ under 70 and where there is a clear effect of the low IQ on the level of adaptive functioning – which has to be at a level or below the level – corresponding to the IQ score. In many countries, there is specific legislation in place for individuals who have a diagnosis of ID – for instance, specifying their rights to special education and assistance in everyday life.

Borderline intellectual functioning (BIF) is a so-called z-code in the DSM-5 (i.e. not a disorder/disease code but a code for "problems" of various kinds) used to delineate problems linked to having an IQ level in the range of about 70–84 in combination with adaptive problems in everyday life. In some countries, BIF is now referred to as "general learning problems".

The diagnosis of ID should be based on an assessment where the individual has been (appropriately/expertly) tested at IQ levels under 70 on two different occasions (usually separated by at least 6–12 months) and where there is clear evidence of everyday-life adaptive functioning problems. It should only be made after combined evaluation by a medical doctor and a psychologist with adequate training, and usually with the contribution of an experienced education specialist. The vast majority of individuals with ID have other ESSENCE problems or other psychiatric or neurological disorders, which makes a holistic comprehensive neurodevelopmental-neuropsychiatric assessment a mandatory part of the diagnostic work-up (and one that may need to be repeated years to decades after the original diagnosis of ID in childhood).

The diagnosis of BIF should be made in a similar way. Currently, there is a trend to make little of or even refrain from making a diagnosis of BIF. However, BIF is almost as strongly associated with other ESSENCE, psychiatric, and neurological disorders as is ID, and many of those who receive diagnoses of autism and ADHD actually have many of their everyday-life problems more strongly related to the BIF than to the "neuropsychiatric" autism and ADHD diagnoses, and it is essential that these problems are acknowledged so that the best possible educational setting and support can be implemented as early as possible.

Prevalence

About 2.5 per cent of the general population of school-age children have ID, but fewer than half of this group receive a correct diagnosis of ID before age 10 years (Gillberg & Söderström 2003). This degree of underdiagnosis is possibly linked to the psychological difficulty of delivering/receiving the diagnosis of ID and the fact that both parents and "experts" know that the outlook in cases of ID regarding full independence in adult life is not very positive.

Another 10–13 per cent of the whole population have BIF. They do not get the diagnosis of ID but even so have theoretical abilities that are significantly below average. Given that adaptation at home and school is usually not provided for this group, problems such as depression, anxiety, and oppositional behaviours often ensue at a rate even higher than in the group with diagnosed ID.

In any society where there is demand for quick and accurate action and adequate reading and writing skills, it goes almost without saying that unrecognized BIF and ID will lead to problems, both in terms of academic achievement and – partly because of poorer and poorer self-confidence – anxiety, depression, and antisocial development.

A low level of adaptive functioning following on from unrecognized intellectual problems is probably one of the most important underlying causes of psychiatric problems and disorder in modern society, but it is rare for this connection to be made in clinical practice. Instead of diagnosing ID and BIF, often the diagnoses made are depression, anxiety, ODD, and ADHD. These diagnoses may well be correct, but the failure to diagnose BIF or ID will lead to even more anxiety, etc.

The results of many different studies indirectly support the notion that the poor outcome in many untreated ESSENCE cases is mediated by "IQ under 85". For instance, in the case of autism, most of the variance in the poor outcome category is accounted for by low IQ.

Unfortunately, there has been relatively little systematic research into BIF in recent years and into the fact that BIF in itself contributes to poor mental health unless it is properly recognized and appropriate educational support provided. In adult psychiatry (and sometimes in child and adolescent psychiatry as well), general medicine, and rehabilitation, the clinical importance of BIF is widely underestimated.

Box 6.1 Intellectual disability according to DSM-5 (intellectual developmental disorder ICD-11)

Intellectual disability is a disorder with onset during the developmental period that includes both intellectual and adaptive functioning deficits in conceptual, social, and practical domains. The following three criteria must be met:

A. Deficits in intellectual functions, confirmed by both clinical assessment and individualized, standardized intelligence testing.

B. Deficits in adaptive functioning that result in failure to meet developmental and sociocultural standards for personal independence and social responsibility. Without ongoing support, the adaptive deficits limit functioning in one or more activities of daily life.

C. Onset of intellectual and adaptive deficits during the developmental period.

Note: The DSM-5 diagnostic term *intellectual disability* is the equivalent term for the ICD-11 diagnosis of *intellectual developmental disorder.*

Specify current severity:

Mild (approximately corresponding to IQ 50–69)

Moderate (IQ 35–49)

Severe (IQ 20–34)

Profound (IQ < 20)

Symptoms

Any "ESSENCE symptom" can be the first signal that the child has ID. In cases with moderate and severe ID (IQ under about 50), there is usually a severe lag in the rate of early development, as regards motor functioning, speech and language, and general cognitive skills.

In cases of BIF, the first early symptoms are often a combination of "slowness", mild to moderate learning problems, and attention/concentration difficulties. BIF usually does not in itself lead to major problems until the child is of school age, and then often presents as a learning difficulty or general behaviour problems.

It is not uncommon for BIF to go "undiagnosed" and even unrecognized throughout childhood and adolescence. In such cases, anxiety problems and depressive and ADHD-like symptoms come to the fore, particularly in the school setting, and it is likely that anxiety disorder, depression, and ADHD will be diagnosed rather than the primary underlying problem of BIF. Maybe even more frequently, teenagers with unrecognized BIF start truanting, and may be drawn into gangs and start identifying as antisocial individuals.

Causes and risk factors

Almost all those with severe ID have one or more identifiable/diagnosable cause(s), ranging from chromosomal abnormalities such as in Down's Syndrome and trisomy 18, genetic disorders such as tuberous sclerosis and neurofibromatosis, toxic/teratogenic syndromes including foetal alcohol syndrome (FAS) and valproic acid syndrome (VAS), through brain damage syndromes after extremes of prematurity, birth asphyxia, and severe brain infections in the first few years of life. In cases with less severe degrees of ID, a likely cause can be found in about half to two-thirds of all cases. The remainder of such cases have ID as a consequence of being at the extreme low end of the "normal" IQ spectrum.

The majority of cases with BIF have low IQ because they are at the low end of the normal IQ distribution. Some cases are caused by damage in the nervous system contracted during foetal life or the early years, and, in exceptional cases, by lack of early stimulation and maltreatment.

Interventions and treatments

Getting adequate personalized education adapted to the individual's level of cognitive skills is of the utmost importance in all cases of ID. The majority of those with severe and moderate levels of ID will be discovered and properly diagnosed and attended to before starting school. However, in the case of milder ID (IQ about 50–70), a correct diagnosis is often not made until well into the school years and may not be made until adolescence or adulthood (or indeed sometimes be missed altogether).

In cases with BIF, early recognition and proper adaptation of the education and training delivered is also very important. Providing a setting in which the individual can be followed up at regular intervals (e.g. yearly, once every three years) is key, not least given the shifting in terms of emotional and behavioural problems that very often ensue over the years. Unfortunately, at the time of writing, systematic educational adjustments are only made in a small minority of this group.

Testing of the individual's cognitive level of functioning is needed before providing adequate educational measures and other interventions. All professionals working with children and adolescents with emotional, behavioural, and/or "neuropsychiatric problems", children who have adaptive functioning deficits and learning problems of different types, need to be aware that the problems may be related to the individual's cognitive level of functioning. A clinical decision will have to be made and, in order to arrive at the best possible diagnosis, a cognitive/neuropsychological test usually has to be performed. If the test results indicate that there might be ID or BIF, a new assessment, including re-testing, should usually be performed about a year later, at least in cases where the first test was undertaken before about age 6–7 years. The re-testing is often needed to make certain that the first test did not over- or underestimate the individual's "real" cognitive level.

Outcome

IQ estimated at more than one test occasion during the early school years is usually a very stable index over time, much more stable than most so-called psychiatric diagnoses (autism perhaps being the only such diagnosis that is almost as stable). Early extreme deprivation can lead to "lowering" of IQ and very early stimulation might "increase" it, but only within limits. The relationship between IQ and academic achievement is strong but by no means linear.

For individuals with ID documented already before starting school, the prognosis regarding a completely independent existence in adult life is relatively poor.

It is important to keep in mind that individuals with BIF have a very much higher rate of other ESSENCE problems than do those with IQs in the so-called normal range. These problems (be they ADHD, DCD, or speech-language disorder) are usually amenable to treatments/interventions of various types, and in this respect they do not differ from the situation in children with such problems who have IQs of 85 or higher.

The outcome for adult life in ID is not only related to IQ and adaptive functioning at school age but also to the associated ESSENCE problems (e.g. ADHD and DCD) and other diseases/ disorders (such as chromosomal abnormalities, epilepsy, and cerebral palsy).

It is not possible to generalize when it comes to outcome prognosis in BIF. However, there can be no doubt that unrecognized learning problems that are not intervened for (educationally and in other ways) at school age will lead to a very high risk of failure academically and as regards social relationships. The risk of being bullied is extremely high. Given the very high rate of other associated ESSENCE problems, it is not surprising that the group of young people with BIF have a very much increased risk of psychiatric and adjustment problems from the early teens and onwards.

Chapter 7

Specific Learning Disorder/Difficulties

Specific learning difficulties have been historically divided into two categories: mathematical difficulties, also known as dyscalculia, and reading and writing difficulties, sometimes referred to as dyslexia, even though these concepts actually only partially overlap. Dyslexia is a diagnostic category that has been used for over a century to denote reading and writing difficulties that cannot be attributed to low general intelligence. The general, increasingly common term "reading and writing difficulties" refers to both dyslexia (with a discrepancy between general intelligence and reading and writing ability) and cases where the difficulties are at least partially attributable to more or less general learning difficulties.

Prevalence

Several per cent of the population have a specific learning disorder/ or combinations of these learning difficulties (mathematical difficulties or reading and/or writing difficulties) that cannot easily be attributed to low general intelligence. Many of these individuals – just like those with general learning difficulties – have other ESSENCE problems such as speech and language disorders, ADHD, motor disorders, and/or autistic traits or autism.

Diagnostic criteria

To be diagnosed with a specific learning disorder, a person must meet four criteria:

1. Have difficulties in at least one of the following areas for at least six months despite targeted help:

    a. difficulty reading

    b. difficulty understanding the meaning of what is read

    c. difficulty with spelling

    d. difficulty with written expression

    e. difficulty understanding number concepts, number facts, or calculation

    f. difficulty with mathematical reasoning.

2. Have academic skills that are substantially below what is expected for the child's age and cause problems in school, work, or everyday activities.

3. The difficulties start during school age even if some people don't experience significant problems until adulthood (when academic, work, and day-to-day demands are greater).

4. Learning difficulties are not due to other conditions, such as intellectual disability, vision or hearing problems, a neurological condition (e.g. paediatric stroke), adverse conditions such as economic or environmental disadvantage, lack of instruction, or difficulties speaking/understanding the language.

A diagnosis is made through a combination of observation and testing, interviews, family history, and school reports.

Types of learning disorders: dyslexia, dysgraphia, and dyscalculia

Dyslexia is a term that refers to difficulty with reading. People with dyslexia have difficulty connecting letters they see on a page with the sounds they make. As a result, reading becomes slow and effortful, and is not a fluent process for them.

People with dyslexia, including adolescents and adults, often try to avoid activities involving reading when they can (reading for pleasure, reading instructions). They often gravitate to other mediums such as pictures, video, or audio.

Dysgraphia is a term used to describe difficulties with putting one's thoughts on to paper. Problems with writing can include difficulties with spelling, grammar, punctuation, and handwriting.

Dyscalculia is a term used to describe difficulties in learning number-related concepts or using the symbols and functions to perform mathematical calculations. Problems with mathematics can include difficulties with number sense, memorizing maths facts, maths calculations, maths reasoning, and maths problem solving.

Symptoms

The first symptoms of specific learning difficulties include difficulties in learning how to read, write, or count. These difficulties are often preceded by speech delay, sometimes leading to an early consultation with a speech and language pathologist, followed by seemingly "normalized" speech development upon entering school. Additional issues such as depression, school refusal, or truancy are quite common (usually because the child – typically undiagnosed and unaware of their problems – feels inadequate and stupid).

Symptoms in late adolescence and adulthood

Children and adolescents whose learning difficulties have gone undiagnosed and untreated are primarily recognized later in life by their secondary symptoms, such as depression, anxiety, school refusal, truancy, and social maladjustment.

Causes and risk factors

Both dyslexia and dyscalculia are strongly associated with genetic factors; in most cases, one or more close relative has similar problems. However, this is sometimes overlooked, particularly among parents – especially when they only have spelling difficulties or something else that might not be enough to warrant any diagnosis.

Both dyslexia and dyscalculia are in most cases likely due to specific variations in brain function or congenital brain malformations.

Interventions and treatments

There are no general treatment methods; intervention must be tailored to each specific case. However, early diagnosis and information, individualized education, and long-term follow-ups tend to be very helpful. There are preventive measures that can reduce the secondary consequences of dyslexia, for example, such as practising nursery rhymes in preschool. Some studies also suggest that learning to read at a very early age, especially for children who are expected to develop problems (e.g. children in families with frequently occurring dyslexia), can lead to good results.

Outcome

No general prognosis can be provided, but there is no question that many with undetected specific learning difficulties (who will thus not get any help at school) will have a hard time growing up.

Chapter 8

Tourette's Syndrome and Other Tic Disorders

History of Tourette's syndrome

Georges Gilles de la Tourette, who was a pupil of Jean-Marie Charcot, described the syndrome that now bears his name for the first time in the 1880s based on his clinical experience as a neurologist working in Paris. He described a triad of motor tics, vocal tics, and "coprolalia" (the compulsive need to say out loud "dirty" words). He posited that the disorder was degenerative and that the patients suffering from it would gradually deteriorate in their everyday functioning. However, long before Tourette, Jean Marc Itard, another French doctor working in Paris, had described a typical case in an important woman of nobility whose coprolalia contrasted with her otherwise refined manners. Itard was also the person who first described a classic case of autism (Victor of Aveyron) in the early 1800s. Even before Itard, typical cases had been described (including during the 15th century) and had been treated with exorcism and gagging of the mouth in cases with coprolalia.

During the 20th century, both neurological and psychoanalytical theories have abounded in attempts to understand the etiology of Tourette's syndrome, and it is only during the past 30 years that the disorder has become accepted as a neuropsychiatric syndrome.

Prevalence

Tics (both motor and vocal) are very common among children during the early to mid-school years, but only about 1 per cent of the population is disabled by the combination of multiple motor and vocal tics, and it is this group that can qualify for a diagnosis of Tourette's syndrome.

Box 8.1 Tic disorders according to DSM-5

Note: A tic is a sudden, rapid, recurrent, nonrhythmic motor movement or vocalization.

Tourette's disorder/syndrome

A. Both multiple motor and one or more vocal tics have been present at some time during the illness, although not necessarily concurrently.

B. The tics may wax and wane in frequency but have persisted for more than one year since first tic onset.

C. Onset is before age 18 years.

D. The disturbance is not attributable to the physiological effects of a substance (e.g. cocaine) or another medical condition (e.g. Huntington's disease, postviral encephalitis).

Persistent (chronic) motor or vocal tic disorder

A. Single or multiple motor or vocal tics have been present during the illness, but not both motor and vocal.

B. The tics may wax and wane in frequency but have persisted for more than one year since first tic onset.

C. Onset is before age 18 years.

D. The disturbance is not attributable to the physiological effects of a substance (e.g. cocaine) or another medical condition (e.g. Huntington's disease, postviral encephalitis).

E. Criteria have never been met for Tourette's disorder/ syndrome.

Specify:

With motor tics only

With vocal tics only

Provisional tic disorder

A. Single or multiple motor and/or vocal tics.

B. The tics have been present for less than one year since first tic onset.

C. Onset is before age 18 years.

D. The disturbance is not attributable to the physiological effects of a substance (e.g. cocaine) or another medical condition (e.g. Huntington's disease, postviral encephalitis).

E. Criteria have never been met for Tourette's disorder/ syndrome or persistent (chronic) motor or vocal tic disorder.

Symptoms

Tics are (to people other than the person affected) unpredictable, sudden, apparently involuntary, unrhythmic jerks and contractions in one or more muscle group(s) – motor tics – or the spasmodic ejection of sounds, noises, words, or sentences – vocal tics.

Tics can be "simple" (affecting only a few muscle groups) or "complex" (compulsive, repetitive, jerky, but almost coordinated movements in several different muscle groups).

The first obvious tic symptoms (both motor and vocal) often appear at about age 6–7 years, but it is often possible to reconstruct that tic-like behaviours occurred long before that age, sometimes even in the first year of life. Head banging, head rolling, extreme hyperactivity, and lack of impulse control have often been present from infancy in those who later receive a diagnosis of Tourette's syndrome.

Often, tics are most obvious and abundant during the years leading up to puberty, whereafter they often abate or become more periodic, depending on increased muscle tension in connection with stress or decreased tension during rest. For periods of time they can be very severe (and be preceded by sensory bouts of feelings of itching, stinging, or stretching of skin or muscle) and lead to major adaptive problems, only to be "gone with the wind" for shorter or even very long periods of time.

Motor and vocal tics can themselves be very impairing with regard to everyday-life functioning, but the most common reason for the individual or family actually applying for consultation and treatment is the very often comorbid/associated symptoms, including attention deficits, impulsivity, and hyperactivity (which are often so pronounced as to warrant a separate diagnosis of ADHD) on the one hand, and severe obsessive-compulsive disorder (OCD) symptoms on the other. Almost all individuals with Tourette's syndrome who consult medical services for neuropsychiatric symptoms meet criteria for ADHD or/and OCD, and need interventions primarily for these problems, rather than for the tics only.

Young children who later get a diagnosis of Tourette's syndrome have often been so impulsive and involved in so many negative activities as to be regarded as cold, callous, and indifferent to the suffering of other people or animals ("scary", "psychopathic"), but others have been timid and anxious, and have shown marked autistic-type traits.

In adulthood, it is not uncommon for the tics to come across only as a "part of the personality", whereas ADHD- and OCD-related problems stand out more prominently and lead to lack of impulse control and severe obsessions and compulsions. This can sometimes be seen as an extreme need for symmetry and compulsive behaviours, such as always straightening hanging wall objects or correcting own and other people's clothes and verbal/language mistakes. This, in turn, can lead to an impression of disinhibition, rudeness, and not being able to listen to other people. Sudden, unexpected vocal eruptions are also common, as are stuttering and vocal interruptions.

The symptom that Tourette himself considered key and diagnostic – the coprolalia – is not typical of the vast majority with the syndrome, even though many have a tendency to express themselves in ways that are considered socially inappropriate and insensitive. In a smaller proportion of cases, "real" and severe coprolalia does occur, and can be linked to sexual fetishism and exhibitionism.

Causes and risk factors

Tic disorders, including Tourette's syndrome, just like so many other problem types in the ESSENCE domain, are highly heritable. This is true also in the case of susceptibility to tics that are not sufficiently severe as to be classifiable as a clinically diagnosable disorder.

One group of tic disorders are probably caused by – or at least strongly associated with – infections of different kinds, or triggered by infections in the context of genetic predisposition. In this particular group, problems are often very severe and complex, including ADHD and OCD symptoms, and occasionally a diagnosis of PANS (paediatric acute-onset neuropsychiatric syndrome) or PANDAS (paediatric autoimmune neuropsychiatric disorders associated with streptococcal infection) is made (see Chapter 12).

It is relatively uncommon for the tics in themselves to be sufficiently severe as to lead to major functional impairments. Usually, as has already been mentioned, Tourette's syndrome is associated with ADHD or OCD or, quite often, both. Autistic features may also be pronounced, and Tourette's and Asperger's syndromes may be diagnosed in the same individual. It is the comorbidity that often leads to major functional impairments during adolescence and adult life.

Many research studies indicate that the regulation of other brain areas by the frontal lobes is insufficient in Tourette's syndrome and that this may lead to dysfunction in the basal ganglia of the brain (which in turn may lead to obsessive and compulsive thoughts and behaviours). Some studies have shown that the frontal lobes grow at a faster rate in individuals with Tourette's syndrome than in those without tics. This has been interpreted as the brain's attempt to compensate for the primary lack of control exercised by the frontal lobes, and suggests that this phenomenon would lead to the increase with age as regards obsessive-compulsive tendencies and controlling behaviour that is often encountered in individuals with severe Tourette's syndrome; the most important functions of the frontal lobes are intellectual, executive, and, not least, "controlling".

Interventions and treatments

Diagnosis and in-depth information (including that tics in themselves are usually not dangerous or an indication of underlying severe disease or risk for progressive deterioration) are the cornerstones of intervention, as in most other ESSENCE conditions. Specific recommendations, such as "collecting tics" for appropriate "ticcing" (in the bathroom or in isolation when other people are not present), often have very good effects, even though there are also cases of tic disorders when such advice is futile and the tics are uncontrollable. Cognitive behaviour therapy delivered by an experienced medical doctor or psychologist can be very effective in some instances.

Tics can be treated with a number of pharmacological agents, including atypical neuroleptics in relatively small doses. However, if the affected individual is not suffering from other ESSENCE problems, it is often sufficient to make the diagnosis, provide reasonable psychoeducation and information that the tics may actually disappear for long periods of time or even vanish completely and never come back, and provide information about the relationship between stress and tics on the one hand, and relaxation and tics on the other. Tics in themselves can lead to muscle tension and head and muscle ache, and other people around the individual might need to be informed in order to better understand the individual's symptoms.

ADHD and OCD in the context of Tourette's syndrome should be treated as usual with stimulants or other ADHD medications, and/or with selective serotonin reuptake inhibitors (SSRIs) and/or cognitive behavioural therapy (CBT). There is a widespread mistaken notion that tics will get worse if central stimulants are used, but the fact is that hyperactivity is usually decreased with the stimulant, and so the tics become more obvious (whereas without the stimulant, the hyperactivity "drowns" the tics). In a few cases, tics do increase on stimulant treatment, but much more commonly they actually decrease, just like the overall level of symptoms (Comings 1995).

Outcome

Tourette's syndrome diagnosed before adulthood often infers that the individual affected will continue in adult life to have a much-reduced threshold for tics of various kinds (including stuttering) and that these will vary in frequency and abundance depending on factors such as stress, relaxation after stress, infections, and other illnesses. Symptoms of ADHD and OCD usually remain in adult life, even though they sometimes become less obviously impairing with time. In a small minority, the outlook is gloomy and the condition might be extremely functionally impairing throughout life (Coffey et al. 2000).

Even in all the many cases where symptoms remain throughout life, there is often good quality of life and both vocational and social success are common. There are many examples of creative, impulsive, and very successful people who have or have had Tourette's syndrome.

Chapter 9

Selective Mutism

Selective (or elective) mutism was first described in 1877 by Adolph Kussmaul (the man behind "Kussmaul breathing" in diabetes comas), although he called it "aphasia voluntaria" (i.e. voluntary muteness). Fifty years later, the psychoanalyst Sophie Morgenstern referred to the condition as "psychogenic mutism", and it was not until 1934 that the Swiss psychiatrist Moritz Tramer established the term "elective mutism". In modern terms, he argued that the condition was an early personality disorder.

The term "elective mutism" remained for over 50 years (including in DSM-III), but has since been replaced by "selective mutism" (to tone down the implication that the child, after careful consideration, has decided not to speak with certain people). There are many popular myths about selective mutism, one of the more prominent being that it is a voluntary way of punishing one's environment with silence (such as in Jane Campion's film *The Piano*). Today, the diagnosis is only given when a child, for some unknown reason, will not speak outside of a specific group of people (usually their closest family) even when they are capable of expressive speech.

Prevalence

Selective mutism appears to be significantly more common in some countries or cultures than in others. For example, a Swedish study from 1997 found that 1–2 children in 1000 met diagnostic criteria, which was one-tenth of the rate in Finland at that time.

Nowadays, the "average" rate is usually reported at 0.5 per cent of all schoolchildren. Girls are affected more frequently than boys and reportedly account for two-thirds of all cases.

Box 9.1 Selective mutism according to DSM-5

A. Consistent failure to speak in specific social situations in which there is an expectation for speaking (e.g. at school) despite speaking in other situations.

B. The disturbance interferes with educational or occupational achievement or with social communication.

C. The duration of the disturbance is at least one month (not limited to the first month of school).

D. The failure to speak is not attributable to a lack of knowledge of, or comfort with, the spoken language required in the social situation.

E. The disturbance is not better explained by a communication disorder (e.g. childhood onset fluency disorder) and does not occur exclusively during the course of autism spectrum disorder, schizophrenia, or another psychotic disorder.

Symptoms

Early symptoms

The condition usually starts as rapidly accelerating "social muteness" towards the end of preschool, but often goes undiagnosed until the child enters school or even their early teens. Thorough investigation of the child's early development often reveals early symptoms that might have indicated autism, language disorder, or motor abnormalities, but these generally tend not to have resulted in any early consultation.

Symptoms in late preschool years through adolescence

The child is described as relatively well-functioning at home, but almost completely mute at preschool/school. Many might even talk quite a lot at home, but say nothing at all or, at most, occasionally whisper in social situations away from home. Catatonia-like symptoms, rigid movement patterns similar to Parkinson's disease, and symptoms reminiscent of "frozen watchfulness" in reactive attachment disorder are common. In some cases, the issues may verge on extreme or pathological demand avoidance (PDA).

Closer examination often reveals neuromotor problems with abnormal results when testing diadochokinesia (fast twirling wrist movement), mild to moderate speech and language problems, and difficulties in attention and concentration. As previously mentioned, pronounced autistic traits are very common and quite a few cases even meet the diagnostic criteria for autism.

Causes and risk factors

In recent years, selective mutism has increasingly come to be considered either a variant of social phobia/anxiety disorder or an expression of underlying ESSENCE problems. Studies from Gothenburg indicate that a very large proportion of all children and adolescents with selective mutism have autism or autism-like symptoms besides social phobia. Many exhibit behaviours reminiscent of so-called catatonia, with rigid movement patterns and symptoms similar to some found in RAD (see reactive attachment disorder, Chapter 11), namely "frozen watchfulness". No specific triggering factors have been established as of yet. Some studies indicate genetic variations and mutations that overlap with those found in autism.

Interventions and treatments

Various kinds of multimodal cognitive behavioural therapy (CBT) have been used to treat selective mutism. Many have reported positive results with significant reduction of symptoms pertaining to mutism or social phobia, but no randomized controlled studies have been done.

Selective serotonin reuptake inhibitors (SSRIs) such as fluoxetine, either in isolation or in combination with CBT, have also been used with moderately positive results. Treatment with anti-Parkinson drugs (e.g. pramipexole) has also reportedly been beneficial in select cases.

Based on personal experience of many cases, changing schools can sometimes and almost immediately lead to dramatic improvement. In such cases, it seems very likely that the symptoms have gradually grown worse in a vicious circle wherein the child's increasingly abnormal behaviour has made the condition impossible to escape; peers continually expect you to be just as "strange" as you have been for many years. Moving to an environment where no one has any specific expectations of one's behaviour thus leads to "normalization".

Out of all ESSENCE problems, selective mutism is one of the most difficult conditions to treat. It requires a great deal of collective knowledge and experience from the doctors and psychologists involved in order to ensure the best possible outcome for the child and their family.

Outcome

There is very little data on the long-term prognosis of selective mutism. Clinical experience suggests that many eventually lose their mutism-related symptoms while the autistic symptoms remain into adulthood. Strangely enough, some end up extremely talkative and "social" as adults, but it is still unknown how large this subgroup is or what might cause such an unexpected development.

Chapter 10

Avoidant Restrictive Food Intake Disorder (ARFID)

Eating disorders with onset in adolescence or later (e.g. anorexia nervosa and bulimia nervosa) often have a background in ESSENCE but are currently not grouped as ESSENCE, mainly because the diagnostic symptoms of the eating disorder do not have onset in early childhood (Råstam 1990). Both DSM-5 and ICD-11 contain a new diagnosis referred to as avoidant restrictive food intake disorder (ARFID); the onset is very often in early childhood, and so it is included separately in the context of this book.

Prevalence

Several per cent of all preschool-age children have short periods of eating behaviour problems without needing professional help or input. The prevalence of ARFID specifically is not well established, but a few studies suggest a lifetime prevalence of more than 5 per cent. Our preliminary studies in Sweden and Japan indicate that among preschool children the rate is at least 3 per cent. ARFID is clearly extremely common in ESSENCE, particularly in the group meeting criteria for autism. Boys and girls seem to be about equally at risk, which is very different from anorexia and bulimia nervosa in which the vast majority affected are female. ARFID does not occur exclusively in early childhood or adolescence, but can occur for the first time in adults – even though anecdotal reports suggest

THE ESSENCE OF AUTISM AND OTHER NEURODEVELOPMENTAL CONDITIONS

that there were problems in early life in many late-onset cases. It appears that ARFID with adult onset may be particularly common in individuals who state that they are "gluten intolerant" (without this actually being the proven case).

Diagnostic criteria and symptoms

ARFID is defined as restriction of food intake leading to functional impairment and need of help and one or more of the following: weight loss or failure to gain weight as expected in young children, malnourishment, need for tube or special measures feeding, and/or severely impaired social adaptive functioning.

There are different symptomatic subgroups in ARFID, including one that involves sensory oversensitivity in the oral region (often associated with general over- or under-sensitivity to stimuli, such as is very typically present in autism), one that is characterized more by stubborn refusal to eat for reasons unknown, and one that is dominated by lack of appetite and slow food intake.

The disorder, although usually commencing in childhood, can appear and become impairing at any age. In cases of the combination of autism and ARFID, the onset of the eating disorder can be in the first year of life and be one of the most difficult-to-treat problems.

Box 10.1 ARFID according to DSM-5

A. An eating or feeding disturbance (e.g. apparent lack of interest in eating or food; avoidance based on the sensory characteristics of food; concern about aversive consequences of eating) as manifested by persistent failure to meet appropriate nutritional and/or energy needs associated with one (or more) of the following:

1. Significant weight loss (or failure to achieve expected weight gain or faltering growth in children).

2. Significant nutritional deficiency.

---

   3. Dependence on enteral feeding or oral nutritional supplements.

   4. Marked interference with psychosocial functioning.

B. The disturbance is not better explained by lack of available food or by an associated culturally sanctioned practice.

C. The eating disturbance does not occur exclusively during the course of anorexia nervosa or bulimia nervosa, and there is no evidence of a disturbance in the way in which one's body weight or shape is experienced.

D. The eating disturbance is not attributable to a concurrent medical condition or not better explained by another mental disorder. When the eating disturbance occurs in the context of another condition or disorder, the severity of the eating disturbance exceeds that routinely associated with the condition or disorder and warrants additional clinical attention.

Causes and risk factors

At the time of going to press, there have not been any well-documented causative or risk factors specifically associated with ARFID. Disgust – as a food-related emotion – has been proposed as a factor mediating picky eating, and it is possible that individuals with ARFID have increased disgust sensitivity as compared with people without eating/feeding behaviour problems. In a subgroup of ARFID, there is a strong link with autistic features, and it is possible that in this group causation might be similar to that demonstrated for autism more generally.

Interventions and treatments

There is currently no one well-documented specific treatment for ARFID, but the principles of autism behaviour analysis and linked therapies often have good effects in clinical practice. In severe cases, treatment of ARFID should be left in the hands of eating disorder specialists (preferably specialists who also have good insights into the general intervention principles that apply to autism).

ARFID is usually linked to other ESSENCE problems or psychiatric disorders (including anxiety and depression), and often also to more specific physical disorders and diseases, perhaps particularly in the gastrointestinal tract. Treatment of the comorbid conditions must take place in conjunction with treatment of the eating behaviour disorder. The diagnosis of ARFID should never be made in cases where the other disorder itself can be seen to exclusively explain the symptomatology.

Outcome

Prospective longitudinal studies of ARFID are currently in progress in several centres, but the results of these are yet not available. Some retrospective studies have been published and results from these are equivocal. Some of these studies indicate a much better prognosis than for anorexia and bulimia nervosa, whereas others indicate a more negative outlook, with some cases having a very gloomy prognosis. Given that population studies of the disorder have only just begun, it is currently impossible to say anything more definitive about the likely prognosis in ARFID.

Chapter 11

Reactive Attachment Disorder (RAD) and Disinhibited Social Engagement Disorder (DSED)

Reactive attachment disorder/contact disorder can be divided into two subgroups: the inhibited type, reactive attachment disorder (RAD), and the disinhibited type, disinhibited social engagement disorder (DSED). Both share the same registration code in DSM-5 (Boxes 11.1, 11.2).

History of RAD/DSED

The Austrian-American psychiatrist René Spitz described "anaclitic depression" in small children who were admitted to hospitals in the early 1940s. Drawing on observations (including filmed observations), British psychiatric social workers James and Joyce Robertson documented the effects of early separation during the 1940s (Robertson & Robertson 1971). Around the same time, John Bowlby – in part together with John Robertson, who he later fell out with – developed his theories on attachment. These observations and theories eventually spawned the clinical term "reactive attachment disorder" (RAD) to describe the (largely unproven) effects of early child abuse, assault, and maltreatment. This term has had an enormous impact not only on social and family services but also on child and adolescent psychiatric services, even though empirical research on this condition has been extremely limited. Now, when more research is actually being done, many of the assumptions about the causes of RAD have proven to be inadequate or incorrect.

Prevalence

The inhibited type of reactive attachment disorder is probably much rarer than the disinhibited type. Counting both types, the condition occurs in around 1 per cent of all school-age children, and perhaps somewhat more often in so-called underprivileged or socioeconomically disadvantaged areas. ESSENCE conditions are generally more common among boys, but the gender ratio is not entirely clear when it comes to RAD/DSED. The inhibited type and the disinhibited type are usually both categorized as RAD, even though their respective symptomatologies diverge significantly (in much the same way that the hyperactive and inattentive types of ADHD are lumped together) (Minnis *et al.* 2013).

Box 11.1 Reactive attachment disorder (RAD) (according to DSM-5)

A. A consistent pattern of inhibited, emotionally withdrawn behaviour toward adult caregivers, manifested by both of the following:

1. The child rarely or minimally seeks comfort when distressed.

2. The child rarely or minimally responds to comfort when distressed.

B. A persistent social and emotional disturbance characterized by at least two of the following:

1. Minimal social and emotional responsiveness to others.

2. Limited positive affect.

---

3. Episodes of unexplained irritability, sadness, or fearfulness that are evident even during non-threatening interactions with adult caregivers.

C. The child has experienced a pattern of extremes of insufficient care as evidenced by at least one of the following:

1. Social neglect or deprivation in the form of persistent lack of having basic emotional needs for comfort, stimulation, and affection met by caregiving adults.

2. Repeated changes of primary caregivers that limit opportunities to form stable attachments (e.g. frequent changes in foster care).

3. Rearing in unusual settings that severely limit opportunities to form selective attachments (e.g. institutions with high child-to-caregiver ratios).

The care in Criterion C is presumed to be responsible for the disturbed behaviour in Criterion A (i.e. the disturbances in Criterion A began following the lack of adequate care in Criterion C).

The criteria are not met for autism spectrum disorder.

The disturbance is evident before age 5 years.

The child has a developmental age of at least 9 months.

Specify if:

Persistent: The disorder has been present for more than 12 months.

Specify current severity:

Reactive attachment disorder is specified as severe when a child exhibits all symptoms of the disorder, with each symptom manifesting at relatively high levels.

Box 11.2 Disinhibited social engagement disorder (DSED) (according to DSM-5)

A. A pattern of behaviour in which a child actively approaches and interacts with unfamiliar adults and exhibits at least two of the following:

1. Reduced or absent reticence in approaching and interacting with unfamiliar adults.

2. Overly familiar verbal or physical behaviour (that is not consistent with culturally sanctioned and age-appropriate social boundaries).

3. Diminished or absent checking back with adult caregiver after venturing away, even in unfamiliar settings.

4. Willingness to go off with an unfamiliar adult with minimal or no hesitation.

B. The behaviours in Criterion A are not limited to impulsivity (as in attention-deficit/hyperactivity disorder) but include socially disinhibited behaviour.

C. The child has experienced a pattern of extremes of insufficient care as evidenced by at least one of the following:

1. Social neglect or deprivation in the form of persistent lack of having basic emotional needs for comfort, stimulation, and affection met by caregiving adults.

2. Repeated changes of primary caregivers that limit opportunities to form stable attachments (e.g. frequent changes in foster care).

3. Rearing in unusual settings that severely limit opportunities to form selective attachments (e.g. institutions with high child-to-caregiver ratios).

D. The care in Criterion C is presumed to be responsible for the disturbed behaviour in Criterion A (i.e. the disturbances in Criterion A began following the pathogenic care in Criterion C).

E. The child has a developmental age of at least 9 months.

Specify if:

Persistent: The disorder has been present for more than 12 months.

Specify current severity:

Disinhibited social engagement disorder is specified as severe when the child exhibits all symptoms of the disorder, with each symptom manifesting at relatively high levels.

Symptoms

The more common type of reactive attachment disorder (DSED – i.e. the disinhibited type) is characterized by intrusive, overly forward, and physical behaviour, including inappropriately seeking physical contact with strangers. The inhibited type (RAD) is instead dominated by "frozen watchfulness" – that is, a tendency to freeze up and become afraid and watchful when meeting new people, as though expecting something terrible to happen. The child is often even strongly ambivalent about interacting with their primary caretaker, with little or no inclination to seek comfort from them.

Causes and risk factors

RAD and DSED are by definition associated with (if not entirely caused by) abuse or maltreatment. The diagnosis cannot be given without establishing that such conduct has taken place or that the child's physical and emotional needs have not been met. However, interestingly enough, at least one-third of all cases present with the symptoms of RAD/DSED *without* any proof that abuse or maltreatment has taken place. Such cases should *not* be diagnosed with RAD/DSED.

In fact, there is no compelling evidence that maltreatment

and abuse cause the symptoms of RAD/DSED. However, there are indications that the strong link between abuse/maltreatment and ESSENCE symptoms mainly stems from genetic factors: parents with ESSENCE problems typically (due to genetics) have children with similar problems and this combination leads to a much greater risk of impulsive actions and "flare-ups" (parents with short temper, little patience, and poor impulse control often react in a rash, impulsive, and unfocused manner towards children who share those same behavioural issues).

The reason that reactive attachment disorder is addressed in this book is that virtually all children with RAD/DSED have symptoms of other ESSENCE problems, sometimes even to the point of meeting diagnostic criteria for conditions such as speech and language disorder, autism, and/or ADHD.

Examination, treatment, and intervention

A child presenting with RAD/DSED symptoms always needs comprehensive neuropsychiatric examination and evaluation. One must not only map out their psychosocial situation but also carry out comprehensive observation, testing, and evaluation concerning all common ESSENCE problems (especially autism, ADHD, speech and language disorder, reading and writing difficulties, and intellectual disability). Parents must generally also undergo neuropsychiatric evaluation.

More often than not, both the child and their parents need some kind of treatment for ESSENCE problems. Measures to address the psychosocial situation vary from case to case, ranging from various kinds of attachment-focused interventions to submitting the child (and sometimes the parents as well) to social care services.

Outcome

The long-term prognosis of RAD/DSED is more or less unknown, as there have been no long-term follow-ups of representative groups.

Chapter 12

PANS and PANDAS

History of PANS/PANDAS

About 25 years ago, the US paediatrician Susan Swedo launched a theory that some children with acute-onset severe obsessive-compulsive symptoms could have their problems triggered by or even caused by streptococcal infection (Swedo *et al.* 2012, 2017). Swedo based her theory on her own clinical experience working in a specialized unit within the National Institutes of Health, where she had seen children who, in the course or immediate aftermath of rheumatic fever – generally considered to be caused by infection with streptococci – developed so-called Sydenham's chorea with odd tic-like motor symptoms and obsessions and compulsions. She named the condition Paediatric Acute-onset Neuropsychiatric Disorder Associated with Streptococcal infection (PANDAS).

Diagnostic criteria for PANS

It has later become clear that many cases with this symptom presentation do not have associated infection with streptococci, and the syndrome is now referred to as Paediatric Acute-onset Neuropsychiatric Syndrome (PANS). The diagnostic criteria for PANS according to the National Institute of Mental Health are presented in Box 12.1. The combination of very acute onset of obsessions-compulsions, tics, or eating disorder plus other severe neuropsychiatric symptoms (including separation anxiety, ADHD-type symptoms, autistic features, and enuresis) in a child who did not have such severe symptoms in the past (even though often mild ESSENCE problems may have been present) is considered typical.

Box 12.1 PANS according to NIMH/WHO

A. Abrupt, dramatic onset of obsessive-compulsive disorder or severely restricted food intake.

B. Concurrent presence of additional neuropsychiatric symptoms, with similarly severe and acute onset, from at least two of the following seven categories: anxiety; emotional lability or depression; irritability, aggression, or severely oppositional behaviours; behavioural (developmental) regression; deterioration in school performance; sensory or motor abnormalities; and somatic signs and symptoms, including sleep disturbances, enuresis, or urinary frequency.

C. Symptoms are not better explained by a known neurological or medical disorder, such as Sydenham's chorea, systemic lupus erythematosus, Tourette's disorder/syndrome, or others. The diagnostic work-up of patients with suspected PANS must be comprehensive enough to rule out these and other relevant disorders. The nature of the co-occurring symptoms will dictate the necessary assessments, which may include MRI scans, lumbar puncture, electroencephalograms, or other diagnostic tests.

Prevalence

There is still some controversy about the specificity of PANS, even though there is now relatively widespread acceptance that some children develop severe symptoms of a neuropsychiatric disorder including obsessions-compulsions, tics, or eating disorder plus other symptoms over a period of only hours to a few days, and that the acuteness of the onset separates the condition from other ESSENCE by the rapidity of the symptom debut.

PANS is probably quite rare and the overlap with Sydenham's chorea is probably considerable. Sydenham's chorea is characterized by motor symptoms that are often expressed as ill-coordinated jerky movements in the face, hands, and feet, and there is also an abundance of neuropsychiatric symptoms of various kinds. This overlap makes it difficult in many cases to determine which diagnosis – PANS or Sydenham's chorea – is the most appropriate. In recent studies from our centres in Sweden and Scotland, we have shown that the symptomatic overlap between the two is quite remarkable (Johnson *et al.* 2019).

It seems unlikely that more than about 1 in 1000 young people are affected by PANS. The male-to-female ratio appears to be about 1:1.

Symptoms

In many PANS cases, there have been mild to moderate symptoms of ESSENCE before the acute onset of new severe symptoms. Asperger's syndrome, mild ADHD, autistic features, mild tics, etc. have often been present for years before the onset (at age 4–18 years) of the new acute and severe symptoms. These new symptoms appear almost of the blue and may be dominated by extreme obsessive thoughts, compulsive acts, and/or acute-onset severe eating problems, catastrophic separation anxiety, concentration difficulties, autistic features that go from mild to dramatic, tics, and psychosis-like, chaotic behaviours with extremes of hyperactivity and self-injurious acts. Enuresis of acute onset is not uncommon.

Causes and risk factors

The exact cause is not known. About one-third of cases have some association with streptococcal infection. Other cases have been seen in the aftermath of mycoplasma or severe viral infections.

There is an assumption that many cases are associated with some kind of immune dysfunction, and about half to two-thirds of children affected have a first-degree relative with some kind of immune disorder (e.g. diabetes, psoriasis, thyroid disease, or rheumatoid arthritis).

In a few cases, the long-term follow-up has shown that the individual has developed a clinical picture consistent with classic schizophrenia.

Clinical assessment and work-up

There is a need for in-depth and comprehensive clinical assessment in all cases and this should preferably be performed by doctors and psychologists working in centres with in-depth and vast clinical experience of ESSENCE and PANS. The details of the circumstances in which the onset of new (and older) symptoms occurred need to be carefully evaluated, so that a separation can be made of "previous ESSENCE" from "new PANS". In-depth history and assessment of infectious agents are needed. In the individual case, the assessments needed will vary. However, it is not uncommon for there to be a requirement for EEG (including during sleep), screening for antibodies against certain agents (e.g. streptococci and mycoplasma), and sometimes lumbar punctures to rule out, among other possible causes, anti-NMDA receptor encephalitis and other autoimmune brain disorders. Specific genotyping tests and special tests for autoimmunity may also have to be performed.

Treatments

There are currently no clear and generally accepted guidelines available as to which therapies must or should be tried in cases with a diagnosis of PANS. However, anti-inflammatory drugs (including steroids), V-penicillin, and intravenous infusion of immunoglobulins (IVIG) should be considered and discussed in all cases. Long-term follow-up and treatment should be monitored by the same team over several years in most cases.

Outcome

The outcome in the individual case is impossible to predict. This is partly due to the lack of longitudinal follow-up studies of representative cohorts of cases with PANS. However, it is clear that some patients are healthy and doing very well a few years after illness onset, while others have recurring episodes of severe symptoms or chronic, debilitating conditions. It is yet unclear how much can be achieved by early treatment, and even exactly what the best treatment might be.

Chapter 13

Behavioural Phenotype Syndromes

There are hundreds of documented genetic conditions that bring about typical or relatively uniform psychiatric idiosyncrasies/ symptoms. Often, but far from always, such conditions also manifest as typical physical changes such as minor abnormalities in facial anatomy, heart defects, or abnormalities in the skeletal structure of hands or feet. Examples of behavioural phenotype syndromes (BPS) include Down's syndrome, fragile X syndrome, tuberous sclerosis, 22q11 deletion syndrome, Noonan syndrome, and Turner and Klinefelter syndrome. Foetal alcohol syndrome (FAS)/foetal alcohol effects (FAE)/foetal alcohol spectrum disorder (FASD), foetal valproate syndrome (which may occur if the mother is on valproate medication during pregnancy), and thalidomide syndrome are also included in this group (Gillberg & O'Brien 2000).

All behavioural phenotype syndromes share several key features: (1) each condition is rare (except FAS and FAE, affecting around 1% of all children); (2) there is a known cause; (3) most specialists that affected families are likely to meet know next to nothing about the condition; and (4) affected families will generally have a lot of valuable knowledge to share with other families dealing with the same syndrome.

In many cases (e.g. with 22q11 deletion syndrome), the behavioural phenotype syndrome is only detected after one or multiple other ESSENCE diagnoses have already been given, such as ADHD, intellectual disability, autism, or speech and language disorder.

Professionals should be aware that at least 1 per cent of the population at large have some kind of behavioural phenotype syndrome (2–3% or more if FAS/FAE is included), meaning that whenever ESSENCE diagnoses (e.g. autism or ADHD) are in play, one must always consider – and perhaps investigate, genetically or otherwise – whether a BPS can be the underlying cause.

Many behavioural phenotype syndromes can be addressed with specific treatment methods. Moreover, assessing risk of repetition in pregnancy and likely long-term prognosis is much easier with knowledge of what exactly is causing ESSENCE in each individual case.

A number of behavioural phenotype syndromes are briefly described below.

Foetal alcohol syndrome (FAS) and foetal alcohol spectrum disorder/syndrome (FASD/FASS)

Foetal alcohol syndrome is probably the most common behavioural phenotype by far, but some researchers and clinicians argue that it should not be classified as a BPS since it is not primarily caused by genetic factors (although they might play a role as well); in more correct terms, FAS thus belongs in the same category as extremely premature birth.

At least 1 per cent of all children have FAS and FASD, and it is probably more common among boys than girls. There is a relatively clear correlation between the scope of the mother's alcohol abuse (accounting for both volume and time) and the degree of symptoms and disorder in the child. However, there is still no compelling evidence that small amounts of alcohol during pregnancy (in humans) cause any detectable alcohol-related injuries and symptoms in the developing child. Children of mothers who abused alcohol throughout pregnancy face much more serious problems than children whose mothers stopped abusing alcohol before the middle of pregnancy.

Typical symptoms of FAS include a distinctive appearance

(small eye openings, small mouth, thin upper lip, small "mid-face"), malformations (heart defects, urinary tract malformations, skeletal abnormalities, and typical fundus changes), cognitive disorder (often general intellectual disability), hyperactivity and other ADHD symptoms, and, quite often, autism. Many children with FAS have a noticeably happy demeanour, while others eventually develop depression. FASD is a milder variant; it does not feature all the typical problems associated with FAS, but virtually all cases meet the criteria for at least one ESSENCE diagnosis.

It is not yet entirely clear what causes ESSENCE problems in FAS and FASD. One complicating factor is the fact that many women who abuse alcohol during pregnancy have ADHD and other ESSENCE-related difficulties. Their children might thus be expected – in part due to genetic factors – to be much more likely to have ESSENCE, regardless of whether they are subjected to alcohol during the foetal stage or not.

There is no specific treatment for FAS or FASD, but one can usually apply the same measures as one would for ESSENCE problems without any alcohol-related injury present. Depending on the family in question, one should, of course, be sure to investigate the biological parents' situation, as well as circumstances pertaining to potential family homes and institutions. Everyone involved in investigation and treatment must have a good general understanding of the link between substance abuse and ADHD (both with regard to the biological parents and the children concerned), substance abuse during pregnancy, and FAS/FASD/ESSENCE, and the fact that both the affected children and their biological parents most likely have complex ESSENCE problems that require individually tailored intervention and treatment.

Valproic acid syndrome

Children born to mothers on valproate (a medication for treating bipolar disorder and epilepsy) have a significantly increased rate of autism and intellectual disability. These cases generally have various types of physical abnormalities as well.

Far from all children born to mothers on valproate develop valproic acid syndrome (VAS), and advising women with severe bipolar disorder or epilepsy to stop their medication during pregnancy is not always an obvious choice.

Neurofibromatosis

Neurofibromatosis (NF) is one of the most common BPS conditions, occurring in almost 1 per cent of the population. Many – but not all – of these cases develop ESSENCE-like symptoms. These include motor problems/DCD, ADHD, and speech and language disorder, as well as autism, intellectual disability, and borderline intelligence.

There are at least two genetically distinct types of NF. The diagnosis is usually given on the basis of clinical picture with skin changes (which can be mistaken for common moles) in combination with benign tumour formation in internal organs, but all families should be offered genetic investigation, consultation, and information about relevant support organizations.

Tuberous sclerosis complex

Tuberous sclerosis complex (TSC), also known simply as tuberous sclerosis (TS), is one of the most serious BPS conditions, at least looking at those who are actually diagnosed with it (roughly 1 in 5000 children).

Benign tumours (which in rare cases turn malign) bring about malformations in both the brain and other parts of the body, thus causing much of the mental and "physical" morbidity associated with the condition. As with neurofibromatosis, many cases show distinctive skin changes.

TSC also has at least two genetically distinct types. Many cases are believed to be spontaneous de novo mutations, but TSC can be so mild that thorough genetic investigation is necessary to establish whether the parents have it or not. There are probably a relatively large number of undiagnosed cases of TS (e.g. parents of children with severe TS), meaning the prevalence of TS is likely to be underestimated. Epilepsy, intellectual disability, autism, and ADHD are almost the norm in small children diagnosed with TS. The cause is a mutation in either chromosome 16 or chromosome 9, and the symptomatology varies depending on the type of mutation. The tumours can be treated, and epilepsy surgery might also be indicated in some cases. Aside from these measures, the treatment is mostly symptomatic and aimed at autism, ADHD, and epilepsy, for example.

22q11 deletion syndrome

Around 1 in 2000–3000 children have 22q11 deletion syndrome. The condition has gained more widespread attention because a subgroup with the genetic abnormality in chromosome 22 develops schizophrenia, and adult psychiatric services often screen for 22q11 in cases of psychosis.

A typical behavioural profile involves speech delay (in part due to the partial cleft palate almost always located below the mucous membrane in the throat), language later becoming the child's strong suit, low energy level, and being "slow to warm up" – that is, a need to gradually get going in order to function normally for a while. While some do have autism, it is vastly over-diagnosed among people with 22q11 deletion syndrome; their languid demeanour in social contexts is often mistaken for social interaction disorder, leading many to be incorrectly diagnosed with autism. In practice, learning difficulties of different kinds tend to create the most issues throughout childhood and adolescence.

Many cases share characteristic superficial features – for example, "heavy eyelids", distinctive nasal bridge and shape – but clinicians need experience in order to recognize features that deviate from the "normal" profile. Many are sensitive to infections during the first years of life. Various malformations (besides the sub-mucous cleft palate) may also be present, along with mild, moderate, and severe heart defects.

Almost all children with 22q11 deletion syndrome have ESSENCE problems – for example, some kind of cognitive disorder.

The average IQ of these children is 30 points lower than that of children without 22q11 deletion syndrome. ADHD and some autistic traits are also common, but full-blown autism is quite rare.

Prader–Willi syndrome and Angelman syndrome

Prader–Willi syndrome (PWS) and Angelman syndrome (AS) have garnered a lot of attention due to the fact that they represent two completely different sets of clinical problems even though the genetic abnormality shares the same locus for both conditions. Although both conditions may come with pronounced autistic traits, people with PWS are rarely diagnosed with autism (Arzimanoglou *et al.* 2018).

Children with PWS usually have severely weakened muscle tone from birth, which can sometimes lead to diagnosis as early as the first few months of life. Voracious appetite and subsequent extreme weight gain throughout the first year of life are also typical signs. Many with PWS have mild or moderate intellectual disability, ADHD, and autistic traits. Quite a few are irritable and also have an almost specific tendency to pinch or scratch their skin. This "skin picking" often leads to lots of scratch marks or bruises.

Angelman's syndrome is associated with a more severe degree of intellectual disability, epilepsy, balance and coordination disorders, and autism with severe obsessive compulsions. Even so, those affected are typically characterized by almost manic exhilaration, paroxysms of laughter, and an exceptionally cheerful facial expression.

The behavioural problems found in PWS and AS are treated – accounting for the degree of intellectual disability – the same way as in other ESSENCE diagnoses.

Fragile X syndrome and premutation FraX

Fragile X chromosome or fragile X syndrome (FraX) occurs in around 1 in 4000 children, but the premutation (the genetic "precursor" to a full mutation) is probably 20 times more common.

FraX virtually always leads to serious developmental problems, while the premutation usually leads to milder (although still quite often clinically relevant) issues (Hagerman *et al.* 2017).

Small children with FraX often meet the criteria for autism and sometimes also intellectual disability. Girls with FraX typically have similar but milder symptoms compared with boys. Typical symptoms include social shyness/anxiety and aversion of both gaze and body when meeting or greeting new people. The intense degree of eye contact avoidance found in FraX is not commonly seen in autism with other causes. Many also have pronounced ADHD symptoms or even meet the criteria for ADHD diagnosis. Some girls with FraX "only" have significant reading and writing difficulties, moderate executive function problems (planning difficulties), or ADHD symptoms.

Premutation FraX (found, for instance, in mothers of children with FraX and affecting roughly 1 in 150 females and 1 in 450 males in the "normal population") usually causes mild to moderate, in rare cases severe, executive function problems and sometimes more pronounced ADHD problems.

As individuals with FraX get older, they often develop growing neurological symptoms, including balance and coordination difficulties and so-called intention tremor (i.e. tremor when pointing or reaching for objects).

There is a great deal of well-developed knowledge about how the genetic abnormalities in fragile X syndrome and premutation FraX bring about the clinical symptoms, but this falls outside the scope of this book.

ADHD in FraX is treated the same way as in other cases of ADHD. A number of medical treatment options are currently being tested.

Down's syndrome

Out of all behavioural phenotype syndromes, Down's syndrome is probably the one that most people are familiar with. The condition is so well known that it is often not mentioned at all in the context of BPS. However, from an ESSENCE perspective one should point out that Down's syndrome is almost always associated with intellectual disability (quite often deep and severe) and that although the "base personality" seems rather "social", the rate of autism is about ten times higher than in the population at large. Studies of autism have often used people with Down's syndrome as the "control group", creating the (erroneous) idea that autism and Down's syndrome are "opposites".

Many individuals with Down's syndrome have heart defects and/or hypothyroidism, which can lead to brain injuries not directly caused by the chromosomal abnormality. It might be these injuries that increase the risk of autism and not the genetic abnormality itself.

Sex chromosome anomalies

In every 1000 children, several are born with sex chromosome anomalies (i.e. having too many or too few sex chromosomes). These include cases with extra X or Y chromosomes and cases where one of the sex chromosomes is missing.

An extra X chromosome in boys (XXY) generally leads to both physical and mental symptoms. This condition is called Klinefelter syndrome and causes early abnormalities in cognitive, behavioural, and motor development, as well as various abnormalities in growth and sex hormones (including abnormal puberty) that require specific specialist treatment. Boys with Klinefelter syndrome often have developmental abnormalities, showing symptoms of borderline intelligence, autism (although rarely full-blown autism), DCD, and ADHD.

An extra Y chromosome in boys (XYY) almost always comes with mental symptoms and often physical characteristics one might describe as "hypermasculine". Many with XYY are more aggressive than their age peers. There is also an increased risk of cognitive issues, particularly intellectual disability and borderline intelligence, but also autism and ADHD.

A missing X chromosome in girls (XO) is referred to as Turner syndrome, and this usually causes a combination of mental and cognitive problems. However, the difficulties are quite often considered to fall within the "normal variation", in which case no ESSENCE diagnosis is given. Intellectual disability is rare, but autistic traits and developmental abnormalities relating to visual perception (including writing difficulties) are common, and delayed puberty is more or less guaranteed. Physical characteristics such as short stature and abnormalities in the skeleton, connective tissue, and muscles are also present in some cases.

An extra X chromosome in girls (XXX) is called "triple X" (older literature sometimes uses the completely misleading term "Super Female") and almost always involves intellectual disability (often severe), complex ESSENCE problems, and various physical and neurological symptoms (including epilepsy). Children and adolescents who have ESSENCE problems and are extremely short compared with other family members should always be considered likely to have one of the sex chromosome anomalies mentioned.

Other behavioural phenotype syndromes

There are hundreds of BPS in addition to those addressed here. Their exclusion does not mean they are any less "important" or less connected to ESSENCE. Some of these conditions – such as Möbius, Williams, Rett, CHARGE, SHANK-3, and Goldenhar syndromes – are virtually always associated with ESSENCE problems, while others – such as trisomy 18 – are so linked to extreme intellectual disability that any broader discussion of ESSENCE is irrelevant, given relatively limited behavioural and cognitive variation in such cases.

Chapter 14

Neurological Conditions and Disorders

Around the end of the 19th century, neuropsychiatry was in many countries a unified medical specialty, meaning that both neurological and psychiatric disorders were considered manifestations of abnormalities in the brain's anatomy or function. Syphilis was one of the most common causes of severe mental illness. Most people today do not know that Sigmund Freud, the founder of psychoanalysis, was in fact a neurologist or neuropsychiatrist.

Unfortunately, large parts of the 20th century were dominated by psychoanalytical theories and "treatments", causing neurology and psychiatry to drift further and further apart. Over the last few decades, we have once again begun to discuss whether neurology and psychiatry should be combined into one single field. The revival of this perspective has been propelled by the realization that many psychiatric problems are in fact caused by brain disorders and that most neurological disorders also bring about mental symptoms.

The most common childhood neurological disorders/conditions that are usually associated with mental or cognitive problems are various kinds of seizure disorders, cerebral palsy and similar muscle control disorders, hydrocephalus, degenerative muscle diseases, and metabolic (including neurometabolic) disorders.

Seizure disorders

Seizure disorders primarily include febrile seizures and epilepsy, but also rarer conditions such as Landau–Kleffner syndrome and Electric Status Epilepticus during slow-wave Sleep (ESES) (Åkefeldt, Åkefeldt, & Gillberg 1997).

Febrile seizures

Febrile seizures are the most common type of seizure disorder and affect around 3 per cent of all preschool children. Only about 1 in 6 or 7 children with fever seizures will later turn out to have epilepsy. Febrile seizures, even when seemingly dramatic, do not typically lead to permanent brain dysfunctions or brain injuries. However, febrile seizures are quite often one of many phenomena indicative/symptomatic of early ESSENCE problems (such as ADHD and/or autism) (Nilsson *et al.* 2016). Children with febrile seizures should, more often than they are today, be screened for ESSENCE, and if relevant symptoms are found, they should be referred for further evaluation and potential treatment of their comorbidity. Children coming to the hospital or emergency clinic with their first case of acute febrile seizures should always be scheduled for a follow-up visit where the physician in charge can assess whether the child has other neurodevelopmental problems as well and not "only febrile seizures" (Gillberg *et al.* 2017).

Epilepsy

Epilepsy occurs in 0.5 per cent of all children. Schoolchildren with epilepsy almost invariably have other problems beyond those included in the diagnosis itself (Reilly *et al.* 2014). While this goes for almost all kinds of epilepsy, so-called psychomotor epilepsy (complex partial seizures) is especially frequently associated with severe psychiatric problems. Motor coordination problems/DCD are also very common, but generally not diagnosed. When assessing children diagnosed with epilepsy, one must bear in mind that other neuropsychiatric problems are virtually always present.

Behavioural disorders and other ESSENCE problems are also heavily overrepresented in epilepsy and probably febrile seizures as well. This link is sometimes due to the underlying brain disorder causing both epilepsy/seizure disorders and, for example, intellectual disability/autism or ADHD.

Landau–Kleffner syndrome

Landau–Kleffner syndrome (LKS) or auditory verbal agnosia is a rare but important epilepsy-related condition that usually manifests around age 3–7 as a loss of speech comprehension followed by speech impairment, often very autistic symptoms, and severe hyperactivity. EEG generally shows a characteristic pattern with so-called Rolandic spikes and continuous epileptogenic activity during sleep. Some children with LKS have clear epileptic seizures early or late in the course of the disease, while others do not have any definite convulsions or seizures. Children with LKS are not rarely diagnosed with autism and/or ADHD.

Epileptogenic activity during non-REM sleep (CSWS or Continuous Spike and Wave activity during slow Sleep) can not only cause LKS but also lead to other sets of psychiatric problems that are difficult to interpret.

LKS should be examined and treated by specialists in neurology and child neuropsychiatry, usually with both steroids/cortisone and anti-epileptic drugs. Prognosis can be good with the right diagnosis and treatment, but tends to be considerably worse without.

Electric status epilepticus during slow sleep

Electric status epilepticus during slow sleep (ESES) – also known as Continuous Spike Wave activity during slow Sleep (CSWS) – is similar to LKS but rarely diagnosed before school age. However, symptoms of language impairment are usually not pronounced or prominent. The clinical picture can be dominated by psychotic episodes, autism, ADHD, obsessive compulsions, confusion, and regression. Recently, many cases of PANS (see Chapter 12) have turned out to be caused

103

by underlying ESES. Most children and adolescents with ESES have no clear clinical epileptic seizures. Electroencephalography (EEG) shows a similar pattern to that of LKS, with long (sometimes almost continuous) periods of epileptogenic activity ("spike and slow wave") during sleep.

Treatment addresses the epileptogenic EEG disorder and includes anti-epileptic drugs and sometimes also steroids. As with LKS, this is highly specialized outpatient care and prognosis can be very good provided that the correct diagnosis is made.

Cerebral palsy and other muscle control disorders

Cerebral palsy (CP) is a clinical diagnosis for certain types of disorders in muscle control and thus also movement. There are many different forms of CP: diplegia (where mainly the legs are spastic), tetraplegia (where both arms and legs are markedly spastic), hemiplegia (affecting only one half of the body), ataxia (where the legs are usually spastic while arms, hands, and torso are uncoordinated/ataxic), and dyskinesia (with strange movements that can be classified as hyperkinesia, athetosis, and chorea).

CP is usually detected and diagnosed at preschool age, but other ESSENCE problems are often not identified until many years later, if at all. Autism, ADHD, intellectual disability, and epilepsy are extremely common (Påhlman *et al.* 2020) and generally treated the same way as in cases without CP.

Muscle diseases

Muscle diseases such as Duchenne muscular dystrophy and dystrophia myotonica almost always come with some kind of psychiatric or cognitive comorbidity, autism being a very common one in both conditions.

As with CP and epilepsy, both the child and the family need the autism and other ESSENCE problems identified as well, so that adequate support and treatment measures can be taken.

Such measures can drastically improve quality of life – even in cases with very poor prognosis, including early ageing and death.

Other neurological problems

Virtually all pathological conditions that affect the brain give rise to a significantly increased risk of ESSENCE problems. This has been shown not only for hydrocephalus and traumatic brain injuries but also for so-called neurometabolic and mitochondrial diseases. The key is to always be aware of the very strong link between brain dysfunction, brain injury, and neurological problems on the one hand, and psychiatric and cognitive symptomatology on the other. Any negative impact on the child's and family's quality of life is often primarily caused by the psychiatric/cognitive problems rather than the neurological diagnosis itself.

Very premature babies are particularly at risk. The vast majority of all children born before week 28–30 will exhibit ESSENCE-related problems before adulthood (see also Chapter 13 on BPS).

Chapter 15

ESSENCE – Three Case Descriptions

This chapter contains descriptions of three cases: one child, one teenager, and one adult with ESSENCE.[1] Each case is followed by a short discussion concerning differential diagnosis. The intent is to convey an idea of the complex set of problems faced by those with ESSENCE that need help, and how important it is to employ a comprehensive, holistic diagnostic view, one that is rooted in the knowledge that all cases with psychiatric problems of any kind, whether they be small children, schoolchildren, teenagers, or adults, may very well turn out to have ESSENCE.

BOY, 4 YEARS OLD (A)
Case description
A was the scream-prone second child of two well-educated parents, both 40 years old when the boy, at age 4, came to his first diagnostic assessment at the local child and adolescent psychiatric outpatient clinic in a medium-sized Swedish town. His older sister, age 8 years, had developed normally and was managing school "without problems, speaking, reading, and writing like a 12-year-old", according to the parents. She was highly intelligent, if also somewhat reclusive, as observed when she came along to her brother's first consultation.

---

1   These case studies are based on clinical examples, but identifying features have been changed.

The father described himself as a happy and open person – "a big-time joker" – whereas the mother, upon taking the son for a return visit (by herself), said that he was probably a "real Aspie". She had a multitude of academic degrees in philosophy, literary science, history, psychology, and anthropology, but ran her own private family counselling business.

The pregnancy with A was "normal"; however, the boy was born after only 28 weeks of pregnancy. He was treated at the paediatric intensive care unit for a couple of weeks and was only allowed home after two months at the hospital. Initially, everything seemed to be going fine, but from the fourth month onward he was screaming around the clock. At the childcare centre, the family was given various tips and recommendations and even medication for both the boy and the parents, but nothing seemed to help until, suddenly, one day, "it finally got quiet". At this time, when he was no longer being breastfed, he instead started refusing food in an odd manner: he would throw tantrums every time one of his parents tried to put him in a children's chair at the kitchen table, except if the chair was placed about 20 centimetres from one of the table corners, in which case he immediately calmed down. He refused to eat anything but puréed food, preferably heavily seasoned. At the childcare centre, his mother asked whether this was normal and was told "Oh yes, you know, all children are different".

Aside from the difficulty in getting the boy to eat a varied diet and his demands to sit in a specific seat, his mum and dad and big sister all felt that A was developing "according to schedule". He perhaps showed more motor activity than other children his age. Without any support, he walked a rather long distance on his first birthday (born almost three months prematurely). At 18 months of age, he had a severe upper respiratory tract infection, after which he grew silent. He had previously said "mama", "papa", "eat", "look", and "lamp", but these words "disappeared". He started to pull away into the corner and rock back and forth. His motor development stagnated, especially his fine motor skills; he could not learn how to eat even with a spoon, but instead stuffed his food straight into his mouth using his hands. He did not help in any way when dressing/undressing. At daycare, staff wondered if it would be best to have him examined as he would often be in the corner by himself, rocking back and forth and waving his hands around. Other times, he would just run round and round for 20 minutes, with no way of stopping him. He had little or no contact with the other children, and the only thing he said was "thisi, thisi". The parents had heard and read that children are so different, and at the follow-up of his two-year prematurity health check, they had been informed that he did not have cerebral palsy, epilepsy, or intellectual disability, so "everything was as it should be". The parents thus did not see any point in bringing him to the 2.5-year health check-up at the childcare centre. Only at the four-year check-up did the childcare centre nurse express her concern about the boy's social development and refer him – after having the paediatrician examine him as well – to child psychiatric services.

At the psychiatric investigation, a young psychologist performed the Autism Diagnostic Interview-Revised (ADI-R), Autism Diagnostic Observation Schedule (ADOS), and the so-called Griffiths test. After that, the child psychiatrist met with the family once and then with just the mother and boy one more time. The parents found out that the boy had "typical autism" and that he would need intensive training over the next two years. They were also informed that his development was delayed and that he might require support at school. He was then referred to child habilitation services for intensive intervention measures one year later (long waiting list, lengthy queue times).

Comments
The autism diagnosis was probably correct in this case. He should likely have been diagnosed with (severe) ID as well, even at his first examination, given that his developmental quotient (developmental age divided by chronological age multiplied by 100) was below 25. "Delayed development" is rarely an accurate term due to the typical absence, as in this case, of any indication that any "catching up" will eventually occur. A probably also had an (at the very least) expressive language disorder, DCD (although his fine motor skills could potentially simply be attributed to his development level), and also ADHD. All of these latter diagnoses would eventually surface in discussions about the boy when, at age 8, he was given a renewed

examination (this time at the child clinic), in which a very experienced doctor and a young psychologist examined him and described that he had a very complex set of problems including "regressive autism", ID, DCD, language disorder, ADHD, and epilepsy. A comprehensive investigation (genetics, MRI, EEG, skin examination, heart and kidney examinations, among others) was then initiated, resulting in the diagnosis of tuberous sclerosis. The psychologist that took part in the four-year health check had noted that the boy had dark hair with a white lock of hair running down his forehead (a classic sign of tuberous sclerosis) and sudden bouts where he'd "sort of stop or come to a halt".

The intensive behavioural therapy that the boy had undergone from age 5 to almost 7 had not brought about any improvements. However, different types of treatment used in cases of tuberous sclerosis (e.g. mTOR-inhibitors such as sirolimus and everolimus, and also targeted treatment for epilepsy, DCD, and ADHD) had been withheld from the boy. It is possible that problems sustained following his premature birth contributed further to brain injuries and the entire complex ESSENCE-related set of problems. One can also not rule out that some of the boy's autism might be explained by the clear genetic predisposition for autistic traits that existed within the family (both the parents and the sister), even though both tuberous sclerosis and premature birth might in and of themselves have been able to cause large parts of or indeed the entire set of problems at hand. The boy's entire set of clinical problems could potentially also have matched an early-onset form of Landau–Kleffner syndrome, but the EEG images, among other things, were not consistent with such a diagnosis.

GIRL, 15 YEARS OLD (B)
Case description

B contacted the children's clinic together with her mother after having had a fainting spell (sinking into a "pile" on the floor) the previous night after dinner (or rather a bathroom visit after dinner). She was extremely thin ("like a skeleton" according to the doctor's notes) and her breath smelled like acetone. The doctor recommended admitting her to an inpatient clinic, but neither the girl nor her mother would have any of it. They were told to come to the clinic the following day. However, they never returned.

Two months later, the girl was admitted to the child and adolescent psychiatric emergency unit with a preliminary diagnosis of "severe anorexia nervosa with elements of bulimia". As she was checked in, her pulse was 44, her blood pressure 95/55, and she was pale and desiccated, with large dark circles under her eyes. She responded in whispers when spoken to, but communication mostly went via her mother, whom the girl constantly looked at with eyes that seemed to say "Come on, answer!", all the while nodding her head in a stereotypic manner and making rhythmic "gestures" with her hands.

The day after she was checked in, a neuropsychiatric consultant came to talk to the mother for 45 minutes and the girl for about twice as long. The mother answered all the questions thoroughly, clearly seeking help, whereas the girl herself only seemed interested in the questions concerning obsessive compulsions, social interaction, and concentration skills. She seemed very nearly indifferent about the whole process and asked several times, "How long are you planning on letting this go on for?"

Another few days later, the patient was able to walk around by herself and move freely within the clinic and the hospital grounds. She seemed to be getting on well and noted specifically that the food was always delivered to the clinic at the exact same time, at noon, every day. Family therapy was recommended as a measure to "resolve conflicts" and to make her stop throwing up and refusing food. Such conversations were initiated at the clinic, but the girl covered her ears and complained about "the complex soundscape" when her parents talked over one another. Her weight was stabilized but not increasing. The parents asked several times about the intended purpose of the family therapy sessions, but were almost equally often met with eye-rolling or shocked reactions from both therapists who also, according to the girl's father, exchanged scornful looks with each other.

111

Comments

The diagnoses of anorexia and bulimia nervosa were surely correct in this case. The girl might also have had autism and Tourette's syndrome; these diagnoses and problem types are common underlying disorders in cases of anorexia nervosa (while ADHD is common in cases of bulimia nervosa), but these have generally gone undiagnosed even when it is clear that they have led to early developmental problems. B might also have ADHD, a common background factor in eating disorders, primarily bulimia and obesity. The underlying problems are necessary to recognize in order to suggest appropriate measures.

Intervention and treatment targeted at ESSENCE (rather than primarily at eating disorders) must be identified and implemented as soon as possible to have any chance of quickly turning the progression in a different direction. Family therapy in cases with anorexia and autism is almost always a contraindication, especially since individuals with autism generally find it very difficult to spontaneously imagine how other people are thinking and feeling – a necessary aspect of social interaction and participation in family therapy. The best option is instead a concrete educational and direct approach in which the experienced doctor, in the acute situation with the potentially life-threatening eating disorder, resolves – together with the patient – to turn the trend around and achieve weight gain within a week, and then, step by step, slowly "shed" the eating disorder and the behaviour associated with it. Sometimes, although rarely, medication can be necessary to break the vicious cycle. In any case, regular follow-up is always necessary for a few years to ensure that the patient's weight is being brought to/kept at normal levels.

The underlying ESSENCE problems will remain unchanged unless specific measures are taken to alleviate potential disorders that they bring about. All studies indicate that achieving/maintaining a normal weight is the most crucial cornerstone of all available measures. Only a select few studies have even addressed the underlying ESSENCE problems, meaning that it is still impossible to say what proportion of potentially negative prognoses for eating disorders can be explained by ESSENCE rather than what is generally viewed as the major acute problem, namely the eating disorder itself.

WOMAN, 40 YEARS OLD (C)
Case description

C had been to the emergency room twice in the last year due to heart palpitations, but her test results had been reassuring both times. She was now reaching out to her general practitioner on account of feeling completely "stressed out" at work and wondering whether she might have become "burned out".

After 20 minutes of consultation, she was diagnosed with exhaustive depression and put on six weeks of sick leave. A return visit was scheduled for five weeks later. She was advised to take it easy.

However, C came back for an emergency appointment after just two weeks, citing huge sleep problems and a need for sleeping medication. The doctor gave her an e-prescription for zolpidem (Ambien) based on information from the nurse who had spent five minutes with C. C came back another time before her return visit due to a migraine attack (something she had experienced on and off for the last 25 years) and wondered whether it might be connected to her exhaustion.

She was an hour late for her return appointment, at which point the doctor did not have time to see her; she was given a new appointment for the following day, but failed to show up for it.

A year later, the woman returned to the general practitioner clinic and complained about pain in her neck, shoulders, lower back, shins, and feet. The new doctor had just taken a course focusing on chronic pain and, after ten minutes, diagnosed C with "pain disorder" and "generalized anxiety disorder". She put C on three weeks' sick leave and recommended physical therapy and gym exercise. C signed up for a local gym but ended up not going a single time over the following four weeks.

Another six months later, C came back to the clinic and asked for advice on her diet, given that "she had put on so much weight". She was worrying about "all kinds of things" and could not seem to settle down at night, merely tossing and turning, thinking about how fat she had become. When they weighed her, it turned out that she weighed just the same as she had done 18 months earlier. The new doctor had recently taken a course on ADHD and started interviewing the patient based on the 18 symptoms of ADHD in DSM-5. C had 14 of them. The doctor also noticed her twitching around her eyebrows and mouth, and that she would suddenly produce strange sounds or clear her throat in unusual ways. She was also constantly trying to adjust things that were slanted or uneven on the desk. In between she kept running her fingers through her hair, trying, in vain, to smooth it out. She told the "understanding" doctor that she had six children who had been born over an eight-year period when she was 19–27 years old and that three of them had been diagnosed with autism, ADHD, or both (one boy and two girls). She explained that the boy with "autism and ADHD" – 16 years old – was on stimulants and that this had been very effective, while the girls had "never had the opportunity to try any treatment at all". The doctor wanted the patient to be tested by a neuropsychologist, but there was no one available at the clinic, and psychiatric services had queue times of more than a year for "uncomplicated" cases.

Comments

The patient most likely has ADHD (her symptomatology is typical and she has children of her own with the diagnosis), Tourette's syndrome, OCD, "anxiety", and sleep disorder. The anxiety might "only" be a manifestation of the inner worry/hyperactivity that is typical of ADHD.

C would probably respond positively to small, gradually increasing doses of stimulants (methylphenidate or lisdexamfetamine), or possibly atomoxetine or guanfacine (these medications are usually relatively successful for the combination of ADHD, Tourette's syndrome, and depression/anxiety). It is not unlikely that she would react negatively to zolpidem and other benzodiazepines, much like many other patients with ESSENCE.

The patient might also benefit from further education about ADHD, and also from CBT and apps tailored around knowledge about the neuropsychiatric disorder.

Chapter 16

A Life with ESSENCE
After Childhood

The vast majority of people with ESSENCE will live long lives. However, untreated ADHD and a number of other disorders and conditions that might cause ESSENCE problems including autism – such as Down's syndrome, Duchenne muscular dystrophy, and certain forms of epilepsy – decrease life expectancy.

Puberty

Puberty often occurs either early or late in people with ESSENCE. Many with autism see their problems intensify in puberty, and some experience episodes of psychotic "breakdown" when faced with stress or a new school/environment. Most of these individuals have a good long-term prognosis as long as one realizes that the deterioration is due to stress and therefore chooses *not* to start long-term treatment with antipsychotics. Others with autism make great progress in their teens.

Girls and individuals with the combination of autism, epilepsy, and intellectual disability seem to be most prone to deterioration in puberty. For some of them, the regression is permanent, whereas others slowly revert to where they were and eventually see additional positive development.

Puberty often brings about some kind of deterioration in ADHD, such as poorer performance at school, development of more depressive symptoms, and/or increasing tendency for antisocial behaviours.

Young adults

People with ADHD and DCD typically seem to mature over a much longer period of time, but this is not the case for people with ADHD and social behaviour disorders. In cases of ADHD with DCD, the psychosocial development and physical growth associated with puberty can continue for many years after the adolescence period would normally be over.

Various types of mental and physical problems – for example, depression (including exhaustion syndrome with depression), "anxiety", being overweight, pain disorder, and fatigue syndrome – lead to consultation with a general practitioner and/or psychiatrist. Depending on their level of knowledge and field of expertise, different diagnoses are made, including personality disorder, bipolar disorder, generalized anxiety disorder, obesity, and chronic pain. Failing to recognize the underlying ADHD problems can often lead to improper treatment, such as obesity surgery in cases of extreme overweight or benzodiazepines for people with anxiety.

People with autism and high or normal intelligence may exhibit very delayed social maturity. However, these cases rarely if ever entail any actual delay; the lingering social interaction disorder simply becomes much more noticeable in an "adult environment" that places greater demands on mutual social communication skills.

Middle age

Quite a few men and women only discover their ADHD or autism-related problems in middle age when their children have been diagnosed with ESSENCE conditions. Tourette's syndrome that previously only manifested as moderate tics and mild ADHD can rather suddenly – for example, in conjunction with infection or stress – deteriorate and lead to first-time consultation.

People with autism often look younger than they are. This might – at least partially – be due to the fact that people with autism have so few facial expressions and so rarely use their bodies for strenuous activities that ageing signs such as wrinkles develop later than in people without autism.

There are some recent theories – partially based on limited empirical experience – that there may be such a thing as middle-age-onset ADHD. However, the more likely explanation in such cases is that these are lifelong problems that only in adulthood become enough of an impairment to seek professional help. One should be especially aware of this with middle-aged women, who may have had lifelong ADHD problems "hidden" behind depression, anxiety, bipolar disorder, eating disorders, or self-injurious behaviour.

Old age

Elderly people with memory problems may sometimes have underlying ESSENCE conditions. In all likelihood, the memory problems in such cases are not caused by any new disorder such as Alzheimer's disease. Rather, the working memory problems (that affect most people with ADHD and some with autism) that have bothered the person since childhood have simply grown more apparent as part of the "normal" ageing process. Typical ADHD treatment can probably be quite effective in such cases.

Several per cent of people over the age of 65 have ADHD. Most of them have not been diagnosed correctly earlier in life, primarily because the ADHD diagnosis itself did not exist until the latter part of the 20th century (even though the problems themselves did, under a different name such as behaviour disorder or anxiety). ADHD being common among the elderly population needs to be made known – not least in district health care services, eldercare services, and memory clinics – if we are to avoid unnecessary examinations and improper treatments.

Sexuality and gender

Several studies indicate that "non-heterosexuality" is more common among people with autism than in the population at large. However, questions have been raised as to whether these studies are truly representative, and the few studies that include more clearly representative groups with Asperger's syndrome, for instance, do not indicate any significantly increased rate of, for example, homosexuality.

A select few studies indicate an increased prevalence of paraphilia in autism. This refers to an overwhelming sexual attraction to trees, boots, or other objects that most people would not find sexually arousing.

Hypersexualized behaviour is more common among people with ADHD than in the population at large. Self-reported asexuality in ESSENCE is uncommon, except in autism/Asperger's syndrome where the rate is probably significantly increased.

However, several studies show a very significantly increased rate of autism among people who have been diagnosed with gender dysphoria. This is something that must be taken into account in examinations aimed at determining whether gender medical procedures should take place before adult age, where it is legal to (Thompson *et al.* 2021, to be published). In the UK, an individual must be 18 in order to have gender reassignment surgery (NHS 2020). Experience indicates that certain people with autism run a significant risk of regretting their decision after completed gender reassignment.

Research on sexuality and gender identity among people with ESSENCE is lagging behind and should be highly prioritized in the years to come.

Chapter 17

ESSENCE Centres

ESSENCE must be considered a public health problem given that it affects at least 1 in 10 families. This means that many families are in need of early examination and support for their children (Gillberg 2010; Gillberg & Fernell 2014).

Children and their families are often not provided appropriate help

Affected children and families rarely get the comprehensive support they need. If any diagnosis is even given before the child enters school, it usually only highlights one aspect of what is in fact a much more complex set of problems. A child who meets the criteria for autism might get that specific diagnosis and all the treatment and support that comes with it, but at the same time have their intellectual disability, language disorder, and ADHD either partially or completely overlooked. This is very problematic, because naturally all of the latter issues might very well have just as much of a negative impact on the child's continued development as autism. Another child might visit a speech and language pathologist due to speech delay and promptly be diagnosed with language disorder, leaving their concurrent problems with ADHD and DCD undetected and undiagnosed for years.

Gathering knowledge in one place – ESSENCE centres

In the future, families should have access to "one-stop shops" where they can come into contact with specialists across the entire ESSENCE field. At a minimum, these must include doctors, nurses, psychologists, and special educators. Other professional categories such as speech and language pathologists, occupational therapists, audiologists, and clinical geneticists must be tied to the ESSENCE clinic as well. Extensive knowledge about child psychiatry/child neurology, developmental psychology, genetics, epigenetics, the brain's early development, family medicine, and education/pedagogy would be essential at such ESSENCE centres.

Comprehensively mapping out problems and strengths can quickly lead to adjustments both at home and school and thereby reduce stress. Indirect results from a number of different long-term studies indicate that this may in turn prevent secondary problems such as low self-esteem, bullying, truancy, depression, suicidal acts, and drug abuse, and possibly even the development of potential eating disorders and psychoses.

Detection/screening

There are various screening instruments (mostly questionnaires or observation schedules) that can be used in collaboration between parents and staff at childcare centres or child clinics of different kinds. Many of these have turned out to be very effective in detecting children with different types of ESSENCE – for example, M-CHAT (for autism), ESSENCE-Q for all types of ESSENCE, SDQ for "child psychiatric problems", and simple language screening for speech and language disorders (Nygren *et al.* 2012). Some of these are available for free online. However, they are not meant to be filled out by parents on their own but rather together with a childcare centre nurse, paediatrician, or child psychiatrist (Hatakenaka 2018).

Box 17.1 Early ESSENCE red flags
Concerns regarding preschoolers' development that call for consideration of ESSENCE screening

- General development

- Motor control

- Language/communication

- Social interaction

- Attention ("does not seem to listen")

- Activity (too high/too low)/impulsiveness (extreme)

- General behaviour

- Mood

- Sleep/feeding

Some people question whether early screening of all children – for example, through childcare centres – is worth it. However, at least with regard to autism, intellectual disability, and language disorder, there is overwhelming evidence that early detection improves long-term prognosis. It is difficult to understand the value of waiting until many secondary problems have arisen. There is no doubt that autism, for example, can be detected much sooner using this kind of general screening, so many countries recommend this sort of early autism screening. Screening instruments can also be used when a child seems to have, for example, autism or language disorder.

Examination and diagnosis

When autism or language disorder, for example, is strongly suspected and subsequently confirmed through initial screening (e.g. at a childcare centre), the child in question should undergo thorough examination in order to determine the diagnosis and map out what kind of intervention is needed. Older children and adolescents who visit paediatric, psychiatric, or school health services and present with mental or psychosomatic problems or eating disorders should always be screened for ESSENCE and – if enough indications are there – undergo a full diagnostic process.

Adults with ESSENCE problems have almost always been given other diagnoses by general practitioners (GPs) or psychiatrists (fatigue, exhaustion, depression, anxiety, personality disorder). ESSENCE should always be considered and screened for in these cases, and if signs/symptoms are found, the patient must be referred for diagnosis.

Diagnosis must be provided by well-educated psychiatrists, GPs, and paediatricians in collaboration with psychologists. A well-functioning ESSENCE team should also include a nurse and preferably an educator, occupational therapist, speech and language pathologist, and physical therapist. Close collaboration with paediatric and school health services, and preferably social care services as well, is also desirable.

The diagnostic process should not just determine whether the exact criteria for a specific diagnosis (e.g. autism or ADHD) are met, but rather provide a comprehensive description of the individual's difficulties and strengths, and thus form the basis for suggested support measures and treatments. A main diagnosis (e.g. Tourette's syndrome) can certainly be made, but must almost always be framed by (usually several) additional diagnoses (e.g. ADHD and OCD). More additional diagnoses (e.g. depression and anorexia nervosa) must also be provided when necessary. Anything that can be addressed/ treated and requires support must be given a name in conjunction with the diagnosis.

The examination process naturally varies from person to person, depending on which diagnoses might be in question. Experienced clinicians can generally determine which diagnoses to consider with relative ease, and they decide which examinations should be done in each specific case.

When ESSENCE diagnoses have been made, one must determine which additional examinations are necessary. All children diagnosed with one or more ESSENCE conditions should be assessed with regard to not only cognitive level and specific neuropsychological profile (e.g. using one of the so-called Wechsler scales) but also adaptive function (using e.g. Vineland or ABAS). Small children who meet the criteria for two or more ESSENCE diagnoses should get cognitive and adaptive assessment immediately, as follow-ups have shown that they typically need significant support at preschool, school, home, and during extracurricular activities.

The examining doctor decides the degree of medical examination (genetic, neurochemical, metabolic, EEG, brain imaging, etc.) in consultation with the parents – or with the patient if he/she is an adult. Many individuals with autism and/or intellectual disability must undergo extensive examination in order to rule out or confirm underlying or associated disorders such as epilepsy, fragile X syndrome, tuberous sclerosis, neurofibromatosis, foetal alcohol syndrome, vitamin D deficiency, and hypothyroidism, to name only a few. The examination team must always include an experienced doctor with good knowledge of the field in question.

The word "diagnosis" means "through knowledge" or "distinguishing". Diagnoses are meant to identify and distinguish conditions, problems, or disorders in order to implement the best possible measures or treatment. If there is no need for help or support, there is generally no need for diagnosis either.

Diagnosis and examination should also include mapping the individual's strengths. This can sometimes be the most important part of the diagnostic process in terms of determining suitable intervention measures.

Interventions and treatments

The ESSENCE umbrella covers a range of different symptoms and problems that may need to be treated or "counteracted" in order to limit impairment of adaptive functioning.

It is important to note that "treatment" can refer to many different things. A distinction is often made between support efforts, intervention, and treatment.

Support efforts are similar to intervention, but tend to entail more general, overarching measures that can be directed at a larger group of children (e.g. all children; all children with dyslexia, speech and language problems, or sleeping problems).

Intervention involves some kind of planned help effort directed at an individual child or a smaller group of children. The measures taken are based on knowledge of a specific problem that one can reasonably expect to alleviate (e.g. speech and language training for speech and language disorder, or slowly increasing exposure to the kinds of sensory stimuli that affect certain children with autism).

Treatment usually refers to a specific measure (e.g. medication or cognitive behavioural therapy) expected to cure or at least significantly reduce symptoms within a set period of time (weeks, months, or years).

The term "treatment" is closely associated with terms like "disease" and "symptoms", while support efforts and intervention involve measures meant to reduce the negative effects of disorders whether they are caused by any underlying disease or not.

Many ESSENCE problems are not diseases to be treated but rather disorders to be mitigated. However, symptomatic treatment is not uncommon. This is used in ADHD (medication for concentration difficulties and hyperactivity/impulsiveness), OCD (cognitive behavioural therapy for obsessive compulsions), and DCD (specifically targeted motor training).

Information for families/parent training programmes

For many families affected by ESSENCE, getting proper information and having access to parent training programmes are the most crucial components of the intervention programme. Both affected individuals and their families need tailored reports detailing the results of examination, including strengths and difficulties. This forms the cornerstone in the multi-year follow-up work that virtually always must be done. Generally, such information must be given on at least two different occasions with weeks or months in between, so that the family/individual can have time to process the information first, and then ask questions based on their newfound knowledge on another occasion.

Parent training programmes concerning ESSENCE can be very valuable when tailored to the issues at hand, but are almost entirely without any specific value if they simply function as some sort of general parent training. "Family weekends" or even "family weeks" – where several families with ESSENCE problems gather (sometimes in a kind of boarding school format) to hear lectures and discuss problems with both experts and each other – can, according to several follow-up studies, significantly improve quality of life. The PR-ESSENCE model referred to in Chapter 2, may eventually become "standard" (Johnson *et al.* 2020).

One must be aware of the high prevalence of ESSENCE in parents and siblings of children with ESSENCE and – when necessary – refer them for examination and additional support as well, rather than only focus on the child with the primary diagnosis.

Informing the individual with ESSENCE

It is impossible to say at what age or point in time the child should learn more detailed information about their diagnosis, but, generally speaking, the earlier the better. Families almost always benefit from being able to speak openly and without fear of any judgmental attitude about the child's diagnosis/diagnoses, difficulties, and strengths (which are sometimes quite significant).

Naturally, one must not use overly complex or technical language when explaining the diagnosis to the child – the most important thing is to ensure that they understand exactly what you are saying. Depending on the child's age, it may be best that the parents are present during all or part of the conversation/explanation. One example of how healthcare professionals can make a child in their early school years understand that they "have" DCD or ADHD is to examine a specific function (such as fine motor skills or ability to remain still) and say something like "I can see that this is a bit difficult for you; these sorts of difficulties are sometimes called DCD or ADHD, which means..."

If a doctor or psychologist is tasked with informing an older child or teenager, a potential description of a specific diagnosis might sound something like this: "Our examinations have found that you have an uneven profile – in [these areas] you are doing very well, but in [certain other areas] you seem to have some difficulties. Would you agree with that assessment?" The answer is usually along the lines of "Absolutely!" or "I know!", which makes it easier to address the whole "panorama" of difficulties and strengths. Of course, some are virtually completely unaware of their underlying problems and view themselves as "idiots", "rebels", or people who have been unfairly criticized. This complicates matters, but as long as one can find the right psychoeducational approach, progress can be made in these cases as well. One of the most important things when it comes to ESSENCE problems is giving affected individuals self-awareness about their difficulties as well as their strengths.

Informing others

Whom to inform other than the child and their parents must be decided on a case-by-case basis in consultation with the family. If possible, it is generally best to inform siblings and other loved ones, either on one specific occasion or in conjunction with parent training. Preschool and school teachers (and sometimes the principal as well) must usually be informed about whatever educational adjustments need to be made. Only then can optimal measures be taken in collaboration between the parents, the child, and the school.

Long-term follow-up

Almost all children who in preschool years or early school years meet criteria for one or more diagnostic categories under the ESSENCE umbrella must be followed up for many years to come, sometimes even into adulthood. Frequent follow-up contacts are rarely necessary, and some cases only require follow-up once every year or two. Ideally, the family should always be able to turn to the same team that they consulted for diagnosis, but in practice this is not always possible.

Symptoms and support measures must be evaluated from time to time. Different problems can be more or less prominent at different stages in life, so one period might be defined by autistic symptoms, another by ADHD symptoms, and still others by learning difficulties at school, tics, obsessive compulsions, depression, self-injurious behaviour, etc.

Making a single definitive diagnosis in early childhood is always wrong. For example, even if a preschool child with autism will always have some autistic traits, their comorbidities (other concurrent issues) will often end up requiring support (sometimes more, sometimes less) as well.

Specific treatment measures including medication

The most common targeted specific treatments in the field of ESSENCE are cognitive behavioural therapy (e.g. in Tourette's syndrome with or without concurrent OCD), speech and language training (including phonological awareness training "against" dyslexia), motor control training (in DCD), and various kinds of medication (especially in cases of severe ADHD). All of these are outlined in the respective chapters.

Public awareness

Promoting public awareness of ESSENCE is the first step towards developing a tolerant and inclusive view of people with neurodevelopmental problems. The first prerequisite for speaking openly about issues such as autism, ADHD, DCD, and Tourette's syndrome is having a name for each problem, as this makes it much easier to find information. While every diagnostic term has its pros and cons, one must still be aware of what they mean and how they are used. That which has a name can be spoken of (cf. Wittgenstein's "Whereof one cannot speak thereof one must be silent").

Everyone who works with children – for example, teachers,

paediatricians, child and adolescent psychiatrists, childcare centre personnel, child psychologists, speech and language pathologists, physical therapists, occupational therapists, child nurses, and other professional groups – must not only be educated in this field but also keep up to date with all its rapid developments. This also applies to adult psychiatrists, GPs, social workers, employment officers, social insurance agency personnel, police officers, lawyers, correctional officers, and addiction treatment personnel.

The best thing would be if children – preferably in primary school – were properly informed on these issues, as this would likely lead to decreased bullying and ostracization.

Endnote

In conclusion, I hope that this book will help spread the word about ESSENCE, one of modern society's most pressing public health concerns.

References

Aicardi, J. (2009) *Diseases of the Nervous System in Childhood* (Clinics in Developmental Medicine) (Third edition). London: Mac Keith Press.

Åkefeldt, A., Åkefeldt, B., & Gillberg, C. (1997) Voice, speech and language characteristics of children with Prader-Willi syndrome. *Journal of Intellectual Disability Research 41*, 4, 302–311.

American Psychiatric Association (1987) *Diagnostic and Statistical Manual of Mental Disorders Third Edition Revised* (DSM-III-R). Washington, DC: APA.

American Psychiatric Association (1994) *Diagnostic and Statistical Manual of Mental Disorders Fourth Edition* (DSM-IV). Washington, DC: APA.

American Psychiatric Association (2013) *Diagnostic and Statistical Manual of Mental Disorders Fifth Edition* (DSM-5). Washington, DC: APA.

Arvidsson, O., Gillberg, C., Lichtenstein, P., & Lundström, S. (2018) Secular changes on the symptom level of clinically diagnosed autism. *Journal of Child Psychology and Psychiatry 59*, 7, 744–751.

Arzimanoglou, A., O'Hare, A., Johnston. M.V., & Ouvrier, R. (eds) (2018) *Aicardi's Diseases of the Nervous System in Childhood* (Fourth edition). London: Mac Keith Press.

Asperger, H. (1944) Die "Autistischen Psychopathien" im Kindesalter. *Archiv für Psychiatrie und Nervenkrankheiten 117*, 76–136.

Biederman, J., Mick, E., Wozniak, J., Monuteaux, M.C., Galdo, M., & Faraone, S.V. (2003) Can a subtype of conduct disorder linked to bipolar disorder be identified? Integrations of findings from the Massachusetts General Hospital Pediatric Psychopharmacology Research Program. *Biological Psychiatry 53*, 11, 952–960.

Coffey, B.J., Biederman, J., Geller, D.A., Spencer, T., *et al.* (2000) The course of Tourette's disorder: A literature review. *Harvard Review of Psychiatry 8*, 4, 192–198.

Coleman, M. & Gillberg, C. (2012) *The Autisms* (Fourth edition). New York, NY: Oxford University Press.

Comings, D.E. (1995) Tourette's syndrome and psychiatric disorders. *British Journal of Psychiatry 166*, 3, 399.

Delorme, R., Ey, E., Toro, R., Leboyer, M., Gillberg, C., & Bourgeron, T. (2013) Progress toward treatments for synaptic defects in autism. *Nature Medicine 19*, 685–694.

Faraone, S.V., Sergeant, J., Gillberg, C., & Biederman, J. (2003) The worldwide prevalence of ADHD: Is it an American condition? *World Psychiatry 2*, 2, 104–113.

Fernell, E., Hedvall, Å., Westerlund, J., Höglund Carlsson, L., *et al.* (2011) Early intervention in 208 Swedish preschoolers with autism spectrum disorder: A prospective naturalistic study. *Research in Developmental Disabilities 32*, 6, 2092–2101.

Frith, U. (2003) *Autism: Explaining the Enigma* (Second edition). Malden: Blackwell Publishing.

Gillberg, C. (1995) *Clinical Child Neuropsychiatry*. Cambridge: Cambridge University Press.

Gillberg, C. (2010) The ESSENCE in child psychiatry: Early Symptomatic Syndromes Eliciting Neurodevelopmental Clinical Examinations. *Research in Developmental Disabilities 31*, 6, 1543–1551.

Gillberg C. (2014) *ADHD and Its Many Associated Problems*. New York, NY: Oxford University Press.

Gillberg, C. (2018) *ESSENCE 2018 Book of Abstracts*. Gothenburg: Danagård Litho.

Gillberg, C. & Fernell, E. (2014) Autism plus versus autism pure. *Journal of Autism and Developmental Disorders 44*, 3274–3276.

Gillberg, C., Lundström, S., Fernell, E., Nilsson, G., & Neville, B. (2017) Febrile seizures and epilepsy: Association with autism and other neurodevelopmental disorders in the Child and Adolescent Twin Study in Sweden. *Pediatric Neurology 74*, 80–86.

Gillberg, C. & O'Brien, G. (eds) (2000) *Developmental Disability and Behaviour*. Clinics in Developmental Medicine No. 149. London: Mac Keith Press.

Gillberg, C. & Söderstrom, H. (2003) Learning disability. *Lancet 362*, 9386, 811–821.

Gillberg, I.C. & Gillberg, C. (1989) Asperger syndrome – some epidemiological considerations: A research note. *Journal of Child Psychology and Psychiatry 30*, 4, 631–638.

Hagerman, R.J., Berry-Kravis, E., Hazlett, H.C., Bailey, D.B. Jr., *et al.* (2017) Fragile X syndrome. *Nature Reviews Disease Primers 3*, 17065.

Hatakenaka, Y. (2018) Early detection of ESSENCE in Japanese 0–4-year-olds: Studies of neurodevelopmental problems in the community and in clinics. Doctoral thesis, University of Gothenburg, Sahlgrenska Academy.

Hatakenaka, Y., Ninomiya, H., Billstedt, E., Fernell, E., & Gillberg, C. (2017) ESSENCE-Q – used as a screening tool for neurodevelopmental problems in public health checkups for young children in south Japan. *Neuropsychiatric Disease and Treatment 13*, 1271–1280.

Helles, A. (2016) *Asperger Syndrome in Males over Two Decades*. Gothenburg: University of Gothenburg.

Jamain, S., Quach, H., Betancur, C., Råstam, M., *et al.* (2003) Mutations of the X-linked genes encoding neuroligins NLGN3 and NLGN4 are associated with autism. Paris Autism Research International Sibpair Study. *Nature Genetics 34*, 1, 27–29.

Johnson, M., Fernell, E., Preda, I., Wallin, L., *et al.* (2019) Paediatric acute-onset neuropsychiatric syndrome in children and adolescents: An observational cohort study. *Lancet Child Adolescent Health 3*, 3, 175–180.

Johnson, M., Fransson, G., Östlund, S., Areskoug, B., & Gillberg, C. (2017) Omega 3/6 fatty acids for reading in children: A randomized, double-blind, placebo-controlled trial in 9-year-old mainstream schoolchildren in Sweden. *Journal of Child Psychology and Psychiatry 58*, 1, 83–93.

Johnson, M., Gillberg, I.C., Vinsa, I., Fransson, G., *et al.* (2020) A randomized controlled trial of a new intervention in Early Symptomatic Syndromes Eliciting Neurodevelopmental Clinical Examinations: PR-ESSENCE (*Journal of Child Psychology and Psychiatry* under review).

Johnson, M., Östlund, S., Fransson, G., Kadesjö, B., & Gillberg, C. (2009) Omega-3/omega-6 fatty acids for attention deficit hyperactivity disorder: A randomized placebo-controlled trial in children and adolescents. *Journal of Attention Disorders 12*, 5, 394–401.

Kadesjö, B. & Gillberg, C. (1999) Developmental coordination disorder in Swedish 7-year-old children. *Journal of the American Academy of Child Adolescent Psychiatry 38*, 7, 820–828.

Kadesjö, B. & Gillberg, C. (2000) Tourette's disorder: Epidemiology and comorbidity in primary school children. *Journal of the American Academy of Child Adolescent Psychiatry 39*, 5, 548–555.

Kadesjö, B. & Gillberg, C. (2001) The comorbidity of ADHD in the general population of Swedish school-age children. *Journal of Child Psychology and Psychiatry 42*, 4, 487–492.

Kadesjö, C., Kadesjö, B., Hägglöf, B., & Gillberg, C. (2001) ADHD in Swedish 3- to 7-year-old children. *Journal of the American Academy of Child Adolescent Psychiatry 40*, 9, 1021–1028.

Kanner, L. (1943) Autistic disturbances of affective contact. *Nervous Child 2*, 217–250.

Kopp, S. (2010) Girls with social and/or attention impairments. Doctoral thesis, University of Gothenburg, Sahlgrenska Academy.

Kopp, S. & Gillberg, C. (1997) Selective mutism: A population-based study: A research note. *Journal of Child Psychology and Psychiatry 38*, 2, 257–262.

Lundström, S., Chang, Z., Råstam, M., Gillberg, C., *et al.* (2012) Autism spectrum disorders and autistic like traits: Similar etiology in the extreme end and the normal variation. *Archives of General Psychiatry 69*, 1, 46–52.

Lundström, S., Reichenberg, A., Melke, J., Råstam, M., *et al.* (2015) Autism spectrum disorders and coexisting disorders in a nationwide Swedish twin study. *Journal of Child Psychology and Psychiatry 56*, 6, 702–710.

Miniscalco, C. (2007) Language problems at 2½ years of age and their relationship with school-age language impairment and neuropsychiatric disorders. Doctoral thesis, University of Gothenburg.

Miniscalco, C., Nygren, G., Hagberg, B., Kadesjö, B., & Gillberg, C. (2006) Neuropsychiatric and neurodevelopmental outcome of children at age 6 and 7 years who screened positive for language problems at 30 months. *Developmental Medicine and Child Neurology 48*, 5, 361–366.

Minnis, H., Macmillan, S., Pritchett, R., Young, D., *et al.* (2013) Prevalence of reactive attachment disorder in a deprived population. *British Journal of Psychiatry 202*, 5, 342–346.

NHS (2020) 'Gender Dysphoria: Treatment.' Accessed on 22/10/20 at https://www.nhs.uk/conditions/gender-dysphoria/treatment.

Nilsson, G., Fernell, E., Arvidsson, T., Neville, B., Olsson, I., & Gillberg, C. (2016) Prevalence of febrile seizures, epilepsy, and other paroxysmal attacks in a Swedish cohort of 4-year-old children. *Neuropediatrics 47*, 6, 368–373.

Nygren, G., Sandberg, E., Gillstedt, F., Ekeroth, G., Arvidsson, T., & Gillberg, C. (2012) A new screening programme for autism in a general population of Swedish toddlers. *Research in Developmental Disabilities 33*, 4, 1200–1210.

Påhlman, M., Gillberg, C., Wentz, E., & Himmelmann, K. (2020) Autism spectrum disorder and attention-deficit/hyperactivity disorder in children with cerebral palsy: Results from screening in a population-based group. *European Child and Adolescent Psychiatry* (online ahead of print).

Polatajko, H.J. & Cantin, N. (2005) Developmental coordination disorder (dyspraxia): An overview of the state of the art. *Seminars in Pediatric Neurology 12*, 4, 250–258.

Råstam, M. (1990) Anorexia nervosa in Swedish urban teenagers. Doctoral thesis, University of Gothenburg.

Rasmussen, P. & Gillberg, C. (2000) Natural outcome of ADHD with developmental coordination disorder at age 22 years: A controlled, longitudinal, community-based study. *Journal of the American Academy of Child Adolescent Psychiatry 39*, 11, 1424–1431.

Reilly, C., Atkinson, P., Das, K.B., Chin, R.F., *et al.* (2014) Neurobehavioral comorbidities in children with active epilepsy: A population-based study. *Pediatrics 133*, 6, 1586–1593.

Robertson, J. & Robertson, J. (1971) Young children in brief separation: A fresh look. *Psychoanalytic Study of the Child 26*, 1, 264–315.

Sadiq, F.A., Slator, L., Skuse, D., Law, J., Gillberg, C., & Minnis, H. (2012) Social use of language in children with reactive attachment disorder and autism spectrum disorders. *European Child and Adolescent Psychiatry 21*, 267–276.

Sim, F., O'Dowd, J., Thompson, L., Law, J., *et al.* (2013) Language and social/emotional problems identified at a universal developmental assessment at 30 months. *BMC Pediatrics 13*, 206.

Swedo, S.E., Frankovich, J., & Murphy, T.K. (2017) Overview of treatment of pediatric acute-onset neuropsychiatric syndrome. *Journal of Child and Adolescent Psychopharmacology 27*, 7, 562–565.

Swedo, S.E., Leckman, J.F., & Rose, N.R. (2012) From research subgroup to clinical syndrome: modifying the PANDAS criteria to describe PANS (pediatric acute-onset neuropsychiatric syndrome). *Pediatric Therapeut 2*, 2, 113–121.

Thompson, L., Sarovic, D., Wilson, P., Sämfjord, A. and Gillberg, C. (2021, to be published) A PRISMA systematic review of adolescent onset gender dysphoria: epidemiology, comorbidity, treatment and outcome.

Waterhouse, L., London, E., & Gillberg. C. (2017) The ASD diagnosis has blocked the discovery of valid biological variation in neurodevelopmental social impairment. *Autism Research 10*, 7, 1182.

Wechsler, D. (2008) *Wechsler Adult Intelligence Scale – Fourth Edition.* Bloomington, MN: Pearson.

Wechsler, D. (2012) *Wechsler Preschool and Primary Scale of Intelligence – Fourth Edition.* Bloomington, MN: Pearson.

Wechsler, D. (2014) *Wechsler Intelligence Scale for Children – Fifth Edition.* Bloomington, MN: Pearson.

World Health Organization (2018) *International Classification of Diseases, 11th Revision* (ICD-11). Geneva: WHO.

Index

informing others 126
interventions for 123–4
knowledge of 120
long-term follow-up 126–7
in middle age 116–17
in old age 117
outcomes 12–13
prevalence of 10–11
in puberty 115–16
public awareness of 127–8
and sexuality 118
support for 119
symptoms of 11–12
training programmes 124–5
treatments for 123–4, 127
young adults 116

febrile seizures 102
Fernell, E. 34, 119
foetal alcohol syndrome 92–3
fragile X syndrome (FraX) 96–7
Freud, Sigmund 101
Frith, Uta 27

Gillberg, C. 7, 8, 9, 10, 11,
    21, 28, 38, 102, 119

Hagerman, R.J. 97
Hatakenaka, Y. 7, 120
Heller, Theodor 27
history
    of ADHD 15
    of autism 27
    of disinhibited social engagement
        disorder 79–80
    of Paediatric Acute-onset
        Neuropsychiatric Syndrome 85
    of reactive attachment
        disorder 79–80
    of selective mutism 71
    of Tourette's syndrome 63

intellectual disability
    causes of 56–7
    diagnosis of 52–3
    interventions for 57
    and IQ testing 51–3
    occurrence as groups of 7–8
    outcomes 7, 58

prevalence of 54–5
risk factors 56–7
symptoms of 56
treatments for 57
International Classification
    of Diseases (ICD)
    and ADHD 15–18
    and avoidant restrictive food
        intake disorder 75
    and ESSENCE 11
    and intellectual disability 55
interventions
    for ADHD 24–5
    for autism 34
    for avoidant restrictive food
        intake disorder 77–8
    for developmental coordination
        disorder 40–1
    for disinhibited social
        engagement disorder 84
    for dyscalculia 62
    for dyslexia 62
    for ESSENCE 123–4
    for intellectual disability 57
    for reactive attachment disorder 84
    for selective mutism 73–4
    for speech and language
        disorders 48–9
    for Tourette's syndrome 68–9
IQ testing 51–3
Itard, Jean Marc 63

Juniper, Brother 27

Kanner, Leo 27
Klinefelter syndrome 98
Kopp, S. 10

Landau–Kleffner syndrome (LKS) 103

Minnis, Helen 10, 80
muscle diseases 104–5
mutism *see* selective mutism

National Health Service 118
National Institute of Mental
    Health 85, 86
neurofibromatosis 94